*The foe claims in error that a philosopher I am.*
*God knows I am not what* he says *I am.*
*But, having endured this sorrow's nest, I ask:*
*Why should* I *not know at least what I am?*

—Omar Khayyam

# HUMAN ARCHITECTURE

## Journal of the Sociology of Self-Knowledge

**?**

**Editor:**
Mohammad H. (Behrooz) Tamdgidi
Assistant Professor of Sociology
*UMass Boston*

*Human Architecture: Journal of the Sociology of Self-Knowledge* (ISSN # 1540-5699) is published by OKCIR: the Omar Khayyam Center for Integrative Research in Utopia, Mysticism, and Science (www.okcir.com, info@okcir.com) and printed by the Okcir Press, an imprint of Ahead Publishing House (APH), located at 6 Hobbs Road, Medford, MA, 02155, U.S.A., tel/fax: 781.874.1448. Copyright © by Ahead Publishing House, 2002-8. All rights reserved. *Human Architecture* is indexed in CSA Illumina's *Sociological Abstracts*® and included in EBSCO's SocINDEX with Full-Text® and ProQuest's "Social Science Journals" full-text database.

**Submissions:** *Human Architecture* publishes both submitted and invited manuscripts as well as the working papers of OKCIR: the Omar Khayyam Center for Integrative Research in Utopia, Mysticism, and Science—an independent research and educational project. Contributors extend permission to *Human Architecture* for the publication of their work in the journal. They retain copyrights to their work and may publish them elsewhere. If the submitted manuscript has been published elsewhere before, written permission from both the author(s) and publication(s) where it earlier appeared should accompany submission to *Human Architecture*.

**Editorial decisions:** *Human Architecture* adheres to the peer reviewing principle for advancing scholarship—seeking innovative ways to meet the need in favor of liberatory scholarly practices most conducive to the aim and purpose of the journal. Selection of papers from submitted or invited manuscripts are based on their substantive relevance and the coherence and innovativeness of their argument in consideration of the mission of the journal. Views expressed in the journal by contributors are those of their authors and may not necessarily coincide with one another, or with the views of the editor, members of the Editorial Advisory Board, or the institutions with which any of the above are affiliated. Authors are responsible for the accuracy and integrity of factual, bibliographic, and referential materials used in their own articles, and for obtaining permissions for using copyrighted material in their manuscripts. Methodological, theoretical, historical, empirical, practical, as well as literary and artistic contributions relevant to the mission of the journal are all encouraged. The primary language used is English, but material in other languages may be included if relevant to the purpose of the journal.

**What to submit:** All manuscripts should be submitted in electronic format. They should preferably be double-spaced in Times 12 typeface., with 1 inch margins all around. Footnotes, endnotes, or reference lists may be single-spaced. In general, authors may follow a consistent bibliographic and citation style of their choice throughout the manuscript. Using the ASA (American Sociological Association) style is preferred by the editor.

**Where to submit:** The Editor, *Human Architecture*, Okcir Press, 6 Hobbs Road, Medford, MA, 02155, U.S.A., tel/fax: 781.874.1448, e-mail: mohammad.tamdgidi@umb.edu

**Subscriptions:** *Human Architecture* is a quarterly publication, published in either single-issue or double-issue formats, all issues for each volume becoming usually available concurrently at the end of every summer. Individual and institutional rates are $15 and $30 for single-issues and $30 and $60 for double-issues respectively. *Individual and institutional subscription rates* per year beginning from the most recently published issue (when subscription order is received) are $60 and $120 respectively. Back issues or additional copies of the journal are available upon request at the same rates as indicated above. Rates include domestic shipping and sales tax, where applicable. For international or bulk orders please inquire for special rates & shipping charges. Make checks payable in U.S. dollars to Ahead Publishing House, and send payments to Ahead Publishing House, 6 Hobbs Road, Medford, MA, 02155, U.S.A. Contributors each receive one free copy of the issue in which their articles appear. Rates are subjected to change without notice.

**Advertisements:** Current rates and specifications may be obtained by contacting the Okcir Press, 6 Hobbs Road, Medford, MA, 02155, U.S.A., tel/fax: 781.874.1448, e-mail: mohammad.tamdgidi@umb.edu

**Inquiries:** Address all correspondence and requests to *Human Architecture*, Okcir Press, 6 Hobbs Road, Medford, MA, 02155, U.S.A., tel/fax: 781.874.1448, e-mail: mohammad.tamdgidi@umb.edu

**Changes of address:** Six weeks' advance notice must be given when notifying change of address. Please include both the old and the new addresses in your request. **Postmaster**: Send address changes to Ahead Publishing House, 6 Hobbs Road, Medford, MA, 02155, U.S.A.

ISBN-13: 978-1-888024-28-9
ISBN-10: 1-888024-28-3

9 781888 024289

Human Architecture:
Journal of the Sociology of Self-Knowledge
Volume VI, Issue 1, Winter 2008
ISSN: 1540-5699
ISBN: 1-888024-28-3

# A Peer-Review*ing* Journal

Contributions to *Human Architecture: Journal of the Sociology of Self-Knowledge* pass through a rigorous selective process with respect to their fit, relevance, coherence of argument, and innovativeness in consideration of the scope, nature, and intended purpose of the journal. The journal adheres to the peer-reviewing principle for advancing scholarship, but aims to design and build new scholarly avenues to meet this requirement—seeking mechanisms that foster openness of inquiry and evaluation; mechanisms that invite constructive judgments subject to free, open, and mutually interactive, not blinded and one-sided, peer reviewing practices; mechanisms that can be employed as widely and dynamically as possible among specialist and interested scholars in the field who value the need for the proliferation of new, critical, and innovative personal and global insights and transformations.

To meet the highest standards of scholarship, liberatory editorial practices need to transition from static peer review*ed* to dynamic peer review*ing* models that de-couple publication from defective pre-publication peer review requirements, and engage in alternative peer review practices that remain open to all those wishing to review a manuscript at any time in the post-publication phase—encouraging expanded and deepening exchanges among scholars, authors and readers alike. They need to invite critical thinking about prevailing and dominant paradigms and inflame creative spirits to forge new scholarly horizons and intellectual landscapes. And they need to embrace the subaltern voices in the academia and beyond, voices of those who have been deprived of cultivating their sociological imaginations through formal scholarly publishing avenues.

*Human Architecture* warmly invites contributors and readers to peer review the articles herein and to openly share their critical and constructive insights with one another in the future chronicles of this journal.

*Contents*

# HUMAN ARCHITECTURE
## Journal of the Sociology of Self-Knowledge

Volume VI                    Issue 1                    Winter 2008

# Editors' Note

## Teaching Transformation

## Mohammad H. Tamdgidi and Vivian Zamel

*University of Massachusetts Boston*

mohammad.tamdgidi@umb.edu • vivian.zamel@umb.edu

**Abstract:** The articles that appear in this issue of *Human Architecture: Journal of the Sociology of Self-Knowledge* reflect the diversity and richness of presentations at the 2008 Annual Conference on Teaching for Transformation organized by the Center for the Improvement of Teaching at UMass Boston. Representing faculty across different disciplines, these essays reflect these teachers' creative and thoughtful pedagogical approaches, their focus on challenging and engaging learners, and their commitment to both excellence and inclusion. The title chosen for this volume, "Teaching Transformation"—one which will regularly appear in the CIT proceedings issues of *Human Architecture*—highlights a two-fold interest and commitment that the organizers and participants in the annual conference have commonly shared. One is to advance teaching as a venue for transformative pedagogical and social practices that empower students, faculty, and communities on and off-campus in favor of a deeper recognition and respect for diversity, inclusion, and social justice. However, by choosing the title we would also like to emphasize that in order to meet the first goal above, it is also important and necessary to see teaching and one's habits and styles of teaching as fluid and dynamic, and not static and established, habitus. To advance transformative teaching (and learning), it is necessary to continually transform our teaching and pedagogical approaches and help one another to do the same.

The articles that appear in this issue of *Human Architecture: Journal of the Sociology of Self-Knowledge* reflect the diversity and richness of presentations at the 2008 Annual Conference on Teaching for Transformation organized by the Center for the Improvement of Teaching at UMass Boston.

Representing faculty across different disciplines, these essays reflect these teachers' creative and thoughtful pedagogical approaches, their focus on challenging and engaging learners, and their commitment to

Mohammad H. Tamdgidi is Assistant Professor of Sociology, teaching social theory at UMass Boston; most recently he is the author of *Advancing Utopistics: The Three Component Parts and Errors of Marxism* (Paradigm Publishers, 2007). Vivian Zamel is Professor of English and Director of ESL Program and the Center for the Improvement of Teaching (CIT) at UMass Boston. Her teaching areas include English as a Second Language, Composition Theory & Practice, and Methodology of Teaching ESL. Zamel has co-edited with Ruth Spack *Enriching ESOL Pedagogy* (Lawrence Erlbaum, 2002), *Negotiating Academic Literacies* (Lawrence Erlbaum, 1998), and *Language Lessons: Stories for Teaching and Learning English* (University of Michigan Press, 2008). She has also co-authored with Eleanor Kutz and Suzie Q. Groden, *Teaching and Learning with Diverse Student Writers* (Heinemann/Boynotn Cook, 1993). Her articles and reviews have appeared in *TESOL Quarterly, College ESL, College Composition and Communication,* and *Journal of Basic Writing.*

both excellence and inclusion.

This first effort in disseminating the proceedings of the CIT's annual conference in published form is meant to encourage contributors to further reflect on and enrich their presentations at the conference as well as to provide opportunities for those not attending the conference locally to benefit from its annual dialogues on teaching for transformation.

The title chosen for this volume, "Teaching Transformation"—one which will regularly appear in the CIT proceedings issues of *Human Architecture*—highlights a two-fold interest and commitment that the organizers and participants in the annual conference have commonly shared. One is to advance teaching as a venue for transformative pedagogical and social practices that empower students, faculty, and communities on and off-campus in favor of a deeper recognition and respect for diversity, inclusion, and social justice. However, by choosing the title we would also like to emphasize that in order to meet the first goal above, it is also important and necessary to see teaching and one's habits and styles of teaching as fluid and dynamic, and not static and established, habitus. To advance transformative teaching (and learning), it is necessary to continually transform our teaching and pedagogical approaches and help one another to do the same.

It is the above two-fold concern with teaching transformation that explains why the CIT has embarked on and continually holds annual conferences and series of workshops, forums, and seminars, where faculty and students continually come back to every year and regularly engage with one another to keep the conversations and practices flowing.

For this reason, it is important to also see this first effort in publishing the CIT's annual conference proceedings as one in which faculty from diverse disciplinary backgrounds share their ongoing reflections in order to receive and provide further feedback on the two-fold transformative process

of teaching. We see this, what may hopefully be a regular CIT annual conference proceedings publishing effort, as another dynamic and ever expanding forum on teaching in addition to the good work faculty have done and will continue to engage in during the in-person conference meetings. The contents of *Human Architecture* are available freely online (http://www.okcir.com), printed in hard copy, and also included in leading databases in social sciences (Sociological Abstracts, SocINDEX with Full-Text, and ProQuest's "Social Science Journals"). This means that those publishing in the proceedings issue will have unlimited horizons in reaching out to a global audience in reporting on and disseminating their local innovations in transformative teaching.

In a section following this editors' note, for readers who may not be already aware of the nature of the Center for the Improvement of Teaching at UMass Boston, the program information for CIT as found on its UMass Boston website is reproduced. CIT will be holding its Annual Conference on Teaching for Transformation in January 2009. The conference will provide opportunities for sharing strategies and exploring issues that focus on inclusive teaching, learning, and curriculum change in college classrooms. Additional details will become available on CIT's website (http://www.cit.umb.edu) in Fall 2008. For further information about registration and the preliminary program, contact Valerie Jimenez at CIT: valerie.jimenez@umb.edu, (617) 287-6300.

We sincerely hope that those contributing to this issue, and more of those who have been regularly participating in the CIT conferences and forums, will use this proceedings publication opportunity to further transform and advance teaching practices that significantly contribute to social transformative outcomes.

Mohammad H. Tamdgidi, *Editor*
Vivian Zamel, *Guest Editor*

# About the Center for the Improvement of Teaching (CIT) at UMass Boston

## MISSION

The Center for the Improvement of Teaching (CIT) is a grassroots faculty-led organization committed to collaborative work on pedagogy across all disciplines and colleges. CIT's mission since its 1983 founding has been to help faculty foster the learning of diverse students within a dynamic urban university environment like UMass Boston, with complex institutional expectations, changing communication technologies, and evolving concepts of academic knowledge and training. CIT has used sustained reflection and scholarship to promote more effective pedagogical practice, a high standard of excellence in teaching, and an inclusive education that engages all students and promotes their academic success.

CIT's definition of inclusion is broad and highlights race, social class, gender, age, disability, sexual orientation, and culture as well as differences in levels of skill, academic preparation and language background. CIT takes seriously the multiple ways that these factors intersect with each other and serve as assets for learning and teaching.

The hallmark and strength of CIT is an active network of faculty, staff, and students who regularly engage in critical reflection and dialogue that deepen and extend a culture of engaged learning, academic excellence, and curricular and pedagogical transformation at UMB. CIT's regular programs include semester-long faculty seminars, public forums, student/faculty dialogues, annual conferences, faculty peer mentoring, and the encouragement of scholarship on diversity, learning and teaching.

Established in 1983, CIT's initial goal was to improve the quality of teaching within the College of Liberal Arts by drawing on the skills and wisdom of UMB's faculty rather than outside experts. In 1989, The Center extended its activities to the university as a whole, and emphasized diversity and inclusion as key components in teaching and learning.

## SEMESTER-LONG FACULTY SEMINARS

Since 1983 over 280 faculty across disciplines and from every college in the university have participated in intensive and collaborative faculty development seminars. These seminars consist of weekly meetings and an intensive pre-semester session, in which faculty from a range of disciplines and across colleges examine and interrogate issues relevant to teaching in an urban public institution such as UMass. The seminar in the fall focuses on a specific issue such as Linguistic Diversity in the Classroom, Teaching Students with Different Levels of Academic Preparation, or Using Technology to Enhance Learning. The seminar in the spring for untenured and recently-tenured faculty provides opportunity for these faculty to work together on issues of teaching, learning and professional development. Since the fall of 2000, CIT seminars have extended their membership beyond the UMB community and now include a faculty participant from community colleges in the Boston area.

## FORUMS/DIALOGUES

CIT has sponsored over 150 forums since 1990. There are approximately four to five forums offered each semester. These forums are

The information included in this section is largely drawn from CIT's homepage http://www.cit.umb.edu to which readers are referred for further inquiries.

open to all faculty, student and staff members of the UMB community. They provide opportunities to share perspectives, engage in dialogue, and to collaborate across disciplines about critical and timely issues. In addition to these events, CIT offers an on-going discussion group each semester that focuses on pedagogical issues related to race, class, gender, age, and sexuality. Finally, each semester CIT plans a student-faculty luncheon series that takes place over the course of three weeks, where students and teachers share their particular perspectives on issues of teaching and learning.

## CONFERENCES

Since 1994, CIT has organized a January conference on Teaching for Transformation. The day-long conference includes presentations and workshops offered on a variety of issues that are critical to teaching and learning in a diverse, public institution of higher education. They provide opportunities for presenters across different educational institutions in the New England area to explore issues and share strategies that focus on inclusive teaching and curriculum change in college classrooms. Traditionally, the conference presenters have included UMass faculty, staff, and students, although the conference has always been open to and attended by members of the larger Boston area college community. Last year, CIT for the first time extended the call for proposals to include presenters from educational institutions beyond UMass, thus expanding the offerings of the conference and bringing in an even greater off-campus audience. In addition to the annual January conferences, CIT has organized several other conferences focusing on issues of diversity as it relates to teaching. Two of these conferences, Diversity and Academic Standards and The Media's Message: Race, Representation and Higher Education were held at the John F. Kennedy Library.

## DIVERSITY RESEARCH INITIATIVE (DRI)

From 1996-1999 the Ford Foundation funded semester-long, student-faculty collaborative research teams who examined issues of diversity, using UMass as the site of inquiry. Participants reported on this work at a CIT conference on Building and Sustaining a Diversity Research Initiative. This culminated in the publication of a book written by *DRI participants: A Diversity Research Initiative: How Diverse Students Become Researchers, Change Agents, and Members of a Research Community.*

## CURRICULUM TRANSFORMATION

In 1990 and 1991, CIT coordinated a Diversity Working Group of faculty, students and staff that contributed to the university-wide acceptance of a diversity curriculum requirement. Diversity was defined broadly to include race, class, gender, age, disability, sexual orientation, and culture. UMB now offers numerous courses that focus on at least two elements of diversity. Another area of curriculum transformation in which CIT has been involved is the role that CIT members have played in working with and mentoring faculty who seek guidance with respect to their own teaching.

## OTHER ACTIVITIES

CIT produces an annual newsletter, *Building Connections*, which reports on teaching and learning initiatives across campus.

CIT created and updates each year A Diversity Resources Guide at the University of Massachusetts Boston for UMB students, faculty, and staff to be used as a guide to diversity initiatives on campus.

As a resource for participants in the faculty seminars, as well as for faculty campus-wide, CIT has developed a library that includes an extensive collection of journal articles, books and videos.

In 2001, an edited volume, *Achieving Against the Odds: How Academics Become Teachers of Diverse Students* (Temple University Press, 2001), which focused on the pedagogical challenges of teaching at UMass Boston, was published. This collection includes chapters by faculty who have been involved in CIT and thus demonstrates the ways in which CIT's work has contributed to the teaching and learning of these UMB faculty.

# Beyond the Clip
## Critical Uses of Film in the Non-Film Course

### Leonard von Morzé

*University of Massachusetts Boston*

leonard.vonmorze@umb.edu

**Abstract:** This essay considers ways of using film in the classroom to facilitate and deepen students' critical interpretations of their culture. Noting that digitalization has the effect of leveling distinctions between textual and visual media, the essay considers the pedagogical importance of understanding rather than abolishing such distinctions, because without them films might be reduced to mere illustrations of texts. The essay considers the multimedia classroom as a space of opportunity, in which teaching students to write critically about their culture becomes more challenging but also more urgently important, particularly with respect to visual representations of race in the contemporary United States. To exemplify the essay's claims for the usefulness of film in the non-film course, the essay considers the writer's experience of teaching students to critique the racial politics of two Hollywood films, *Flower Drum Song* and *Crash*.

The digitalization of film over the last decade has not only put enormous repositories of video at our fingertips but has also made film easy to customize for classroom use. Not too long ago, the teacher's use of film was limited to the occasional "movie day," and if you were a teacher of literature, this was generally an adaptation of some piece of fiction on the syllabus. Such an approach to course design seems antiquated today, if not downright stuffy. Free software, a DVD drive, and a broadband connection now make it possible for the teacher to become a sort of disc jockey, spinning video into the classroom experience with as much facility as a line of verse.

Such a classroom experience, meticulously constructed from the materials of short film clips and other electronic media, is attractive because it includes a sort of built-in defensive mechanism against the risks of committing much class time to showing films. If the film is on the computer, all the better: we feel that we are doing more with it. Our suspicion of film runs even deeper. While we tend to assume that our culture has recently grown more fixated on visual media, the transformation of film into another branch of information technology has tended to undercut any kind of breathless fascination with the world on film that we might still have.

Leonard von Morzé is Assistant Professor of English at UMass Boston, where he teaches American literature and culture. His research and teaching focus on the eighteenth century, but he also regularly teaches a seminar for first-year students on "Race and Ethnicity in 20th-Century U.S. Literature." His work has appeared in *Early American Studies* and *Teaching the Transatlantic Eighteenth Century*. He is currently working on a book on ethnicity and political radicalism in the literature of the early United States.

Anti-visual models of Western education that have been around since Plato also retain their influence. Inculcating suspicion of what we see and show, we wish somehow to integrate film with the traditional commitment to the verbal dialectic, and digitalizing film appears to give us a way to do this. It is not merely the development of new technology, in other words, that has turned us away from entire films and toward clips; it is the entry of film into the teaching repertoire of faculty who are excited by its possibilities yet remain puzzled about how to use it.

Let me cite myself as an example. As a teacher with a special interest in questions of race in U.S. literature, I always consider it important to address questions of visuality such as the invisibility or hypervisibility of people of color. In my first-year seminar on "Race and Ethnicity in Twentieth-Century U.S. Literature," I press this theme further, considering it a matter of simple intellectual honesty to teach students approaches to visual representation, without which they may neither be equipped to confront the ever more subtle racism pervading contemporary American culture nor to appreciate the challenges to it coming not only from great literature but film. Yet my training as a scholar of texts (and eighteenth-century ones at that) does not always help me to teach film, since there is no simple analogy between the decoding of visual representation and the interpretation of a text.

I once believed that when I examined film clips with my class, I could approximate the effect of explicating a passage from a text. Yet when I tried to apply the same pedagogic methods to film as I had to texts, I recognized that clips do not offer a true equivalent to quotations, and that I could not plan the same activities with the former as I had with the latter. It wouldn't do, I found, to break students into groups to break down clips (even were this technologically feasible) with the same instruc-

tions they might be given when I asked them to analyze quotations.

It is true that a cleverly chosen clip can provide an arresting transition to arguments about the social function of literature. David Henkin, a model professor during my graduate training, once illustrated the complex relationship of social class to professional identity by extracting a few scenes from the 1999 satire *Office Space*, then asking students to compare them to conditions of white-collar labor in Melville's "Bartleby the Scrivener." A colleague, Susan Tomlinson, uses an episode of *Law & Order* to facilitate rich discussions of the connection between race and class in Harriet Jacobs's *Incidents in the Life of a Slave Girl*. While impressing me with their ingenuity, these mentors have communicated their recognition that the juxtaposition of movie clips with a piece of literature under discussion needs not only to be clever but to foster student interpretation. Extracts from film need to do more than "work" with the assigned readings; in the cases of Henkin and Tomlinson, they provide fresh avenues into class discussion of a text. Presentation of a clip, no matter how smart, does not automatically produce student discussion; quite on the contrary, it has sometimes tended to forestall student contributions, and frustration overcame the more fleeting satisfaction of feeling more hip. How should we teach film in the classroom if we wish to foster active student engagement, rather than a passive admiration of either the visual medium or the professor's technical virtuosity?

My answer is to embrace the risk of offering the class movies on their own terms, asking that students interpret the material *as* film. The radicalism of this proposition entails the understanding that films cannot, as my colleague Linda Dittmar once insisted, be seen as mere "illustrations" of texts. To the extent that teachers see film merely as illustrating some point made in assigned readings, we miss half of their pedagogic value, which derives from the movement back from the text to the film, which can serve as the basis for an interpretive text students produce *about* the film. The model for the latter text can be an exercise that invites students to recognize that they are *already* interpreting films as they view them. What happens to our initial impressions, I ask students, when we view a film again, or just a clip that I have selected from it? With the assumption that students' ability to understand film is a starting-point rather than an ever-postponed end goal, I identify their writing project as the discovery of a vocabulary to articulate and test their interpretations, comparing initial reactions to an entire film with their later analysis of small clips from it.[1]

Seeing the articulate student, rather than the "competent" one, as the measure of my success as a teacher, I teach film theory only as a means toward initiating student writing projects. For reasons both obvious and obscure that I will discuss in a moment, the relation between theory and practice is different in film pedagogy than in the teaching of literature. First-year college students might be sometimes surprised to learn of the very existence of a body of scholarship about film,[2] yet they are usually receptive to a discussion of directorial technique. This perhaps surprising phenomenon reflects the fact that the boundary between theory and practice in film studies is *different from* the boundary in the study of writing, and teachers must ac-

cordingly break this stultifying boundary in a different way when we introduce a film. While we expect students to show verbal acuity in interpreting course readings, we don't ask them to demonstrate their understanding of films by showing that they can make them themselves. Consequently, overcoming the dichotomy of theory and practice in film studies does not mean that we ask them to create a film, but instead to step out of the role of passive audience and to imagine themselves in the position of the director, where they can recognize the techniques at a director's disposal, and understand yet also critique the choices that director has made. This is often best modeled on small selections from the film, but it can help to begin with a more general presentation on technique, which can lead naturally into a discussion of the theory and politics of film. A PowerPoint introduction to film technique constitutes a foundational activity in my "Race and Ethnicity" classroom. While this introduction is by necessity much more staged than subsequent activities, it does not turn students off, for the simple reason that understanding what anyone can do behind a camera is not difficult—which is not to say that anyone can make a great film, only that understanding technique allows us to escape passive spectatorship. (This also happens to be related to the reason I do *not* teach writing as technique, an approach which tends to be alienating and intimidating—a key difference between film and literature pedagogies.)

Discussions of film technique are readily available in many textbooks, but I prefer to host most such discussions in class, because the film medium lends itself well to interactive learning. For example, students may be invited to consider how variations on a shot change its meaning. Drawing on terms and examples from Louis Giannetti's *Understanding Film*, I give students a small glimpse of the universe of alternative possibilities within every decision made by a director. If teachers are tech-

---

[1] Here I draw on Jacques Rancière's radical gestures toward an egalitarian classroom in *The Ignorant Schoolmaster: Five Lessons in Intellectual Emancipation*, trans. Kristin Ross (Stanford, CA: Stanford University Press, 1991).

[2] If necessary, a teacher might mention to students a few striking tidbits from Dana Polan's history of film pedagogy, which testifies to the little-known fact that film has been taught and studied in U.S. universities longer than American literature has been. See Polan's *Scenes of Instruction: The Beginnings of the U.S. Study of Film* (Berkeley: University of California Press, 2007).

savvy, film stills can be tweaked even in PowerPoint to make very simple adjustments to the image displayed, adjustments that might involve framing (zooming in on a small part of an image), angle and composition (reversing or rotating an image), color, and so forth ... and of course confident teachers might also invite students to the front of the class to do the experimenting themselves.

Yet no such technical fireworks are needed to demonstrate how shots convey meaning. While imparting some basic film vocabulary can make students' analysis more precise, focusing their attention on core threads in the course isolates those qualities of form and politics that produce interesting grounds for comparison. In my race and ethnicity course, I ask students to analyze several Hollywood films, two of which (*Flower Drum Song*, 1961, and *Crash*, 2004) provide strikingly different versions of the continuing U.S. concern with *e pluribus unum*. Short assignments facilitate engagement with the films as we view them, such as a written response to a musical number of their choosing in *Drum Song* and a movie review of *Crash* that refers at least two of the ten published reviews I have asked students to examine.

But when I return to the two movies near the end of the course as part of a larger essay assignment on film, I put clips from the films side by side in order to elicit comparative analysis of technique. Such juxtapositions were intended to surprise students, since the two films could hardly be more different. *Drum Song* is perhaps less remembered today as a Hollywood breakthrough (featuring for the first time a complete ensemble of Asian-American actors) than as a fluffy and patronizing account of San Francisco's Chinatown after World War II, while *Crash* remains widely regarded as an earnest and responsible meditation on racial prejudice in twenty-first-century Los Angeles. While *Drum Song* tells a story of cultural assimilation

against a backdrop of segregation which it largely takes for granted, *Crash* presents an opposite vision which assumes a context of integration, a world in which racial boundaries are crossed repeatedly and as though by chance.[3] Whereas the casting of *Drum Song* reveals a reckless indifference to ethnic particularity, the atomizing effect of "political correctness" on *Crash* is to produce a "myopic focus on geographically specific ethnic origins, which [...] dismisses any identities or alliances that transcend these groupings."[4]

By this point in the course, each film has gotten close attention in turn, but the larger payoff comes from considering them in relation to one another. To focus our discussion, we view one scene from each picture side-by-side a few times. In the case of *Flower Drum Song* and *Crash*, I pick Auntie Liang's citizenship ceremony followed by the "Chop Suey" musical number, and Officer Hanson's tragic shooting of Peter in the San Fernando Valley. While viewing the two scenes, I ask students to complete a chart in which they must describe the Mood, Context, and several aspects of the Form of each scene, with no mention yet of the language (dialogue or lyrics or voiceover) of the scene. Sound should nonetheless not be muted, because attending to music provides an important nonverbal expression of meaning.[5] The effectiveness of this activity depends on isolating the scenes, postponing discussion of language, and paying close attention to all of the other categories of analysis we derived from Giannetti's text. On their charts, I ask students first to describe the Mood of each scene, which generates obvious contrasts

---

[3] In this sense, *Crash* reflects the underlying assumption that segregation and an attendant automobile culture cannot keep a diverse range of individuals from meeting in their daily lives—a hope that might surprise observers of contemporary L.A.

[4] Hsuan L. Hsu, "Racial Privacy, the L.A. Ensemble Films, and Paul Haggis's *Crash*," *Film Criticism* 31.1-2 (Fall-Winter 2006): 145.

such as Euphoria versus Depression. A second item, Context, helps to provide greater understanding of the mood: in *Flower Drum Song*, euphoria because Auntie Liang serves as model American citizen; in *Crash*, shock and disillusionment because the lone anti-racist in the white police force has made a horrific misjudgment of his authentically sympathetic passenger.

Yet since I have required students to list similarities between the two scenes, they are forced to turn to features of cinematic form, where surprising connections begin to emerge. In considering music, for example, students readily see that "Chop Suey" the song is, as the elderly Chinese man Master Wang says, a mix of everything, and this leads to the recognition that chop suey the dish, an American invention once commonly accepted as authentically Chinese, offers a satirical alternative to the melting pot as a metaphor of Americanization. The musical score provides an objective correlative to the dish, swinging wildly from one time signature to another, attempting to fuse musical styles that remain basically incompatible. And this of course is exactly how the scene from *Crash* works: it begins with a folk song which has been set to a modern electronic score. Of course, students won't recognize the folk song's language—it's Welsh—or what the voice sings about, which is "Negligence." The opening Welsh electronica sets up a very different kind of folk song, Merle Haggard's "Swinging Doors." The improbable meeting of folk styles matches, of course, the improbable

---

[5] I might note that a similar inattention to language can be helpful even in teaching literary texts. To illustrate the rewards of examining form, my friend Rachel Meyer liked to suspend the semantic function of language by asking non-German-speaking students to speculate about the subject of Paul Celan's great poem "Todesfuge" after seeing it on the page and hearing it read aloud in its original language. Students are surprised to discover that they can produce ingenious interpretations of the poem, reinforcing a useful lesson about the way that semantics are but one aspect of meaning.

encounter of cop and hitchhiker on a snowy night in L.A.'s San Fernando Valley. The principle underlying the use of musical styles in each clip reveal a similarity in their conceptions of the way in which many become one, but they appear to do so to opposite effect: *Drum Song* would appear to stand for harmonious integration, and *Crash* for a vicious separation.

We then consider such formal features as type of Shot and Color Composition. Shot seems particularly important in interpreting the scene in *Crash*, which begins the scene by constructing an opposition between inside and outside the automobiles through a mix of close-ups and longer shots. This leads up to the crucial moment when the director silences the music and takes us outside the car for a middle shot where, in a blinding flash of light, we see the gun going off.

As my student Sarah Hodges astutely noticed, this change of shot is absolutely crucial to the meaning of the scene. The fact that the act of violence is not directly rendered because we are viewing it from a disembodied position instills a sense of tragic inevitability. The film would, in effect, ask us to see the killing as just another black man being shot on the highway.

Now, as the discussion took us toward a careful analysis of form, the class begins to develop a sense of the racial politics of the two films, one that is quite different from where we had started. Students had begun by seeing *Flower Drum Song* as hokey in its view of race, and full of offensive Asian stereotypes, which it certainly is, while *Crash* seems unsparingly realistic, which it also to some extent is. Now these first impressions begin to be revised, and the very simple contrast between the two films becomes more complex.

At this point I invite the students to begin talking about words, about dialogue and lyrics. We look at the actual language of the song from *Flower Drum Song*, and the film seems to put the idea of Americaniza-

Figure: Officer Hansen's gun is fired, killing his hitchhiking passenger in *Crash* (2004). Still taken from *Crash* provided through the courtesy of Lionsgate Films.

tion in a deeply ironic light, as though to endorse Master Wang's dismissal of the citizenship ceremony, his conviction that chop suey is so much "bally hooey":

> *Living here is very much like chop suey.*
> *Hula hoops and nuclear war,*
> *Doctor Salk and Zsa Zsa Gabor,*
> *Bobby Darin, Sandra Dee, and Dewey,*
> *Chop suey, chop suey!*
>
> ..........
>
> *Mixed with all the hokum and bally hooey.*
> *Something real and glowing grand.*
> *Sheds a light all over the land.*
> *Chop suey, chop suey!*

Students now see that all this apparent jubilation harbors an underlying bitterness at the forms of disenfranchisement that paradoxically accompany Auntie Liang's new American identity. As Anne Cheng suggests, the musical genre is well suited to *Flower Drum Song*'s expressions of "pathological euphoria," a compulsively manic, manufactured glee on the part of an Asian-American community which serves as psychic compensation for the grief that came from decades of exclusion.[6] When the cho-

rus claims that "something real and glowing grand" underlies their new American identity, they protest too much. The "real" might also reflect the terrors of the Cold War. As the unlikely origins of the word "bikini" in the horror of atomic testing might suggest, the phrase "hula hoops and nuclear war" is an appropriate way of identifying the historical conjuncture of titillation and terror.

As their short responses to these two clips revealed, attention to cinematic technique can facilitate students' understanding of the theory and politics of film. While several students had initially found *Crash* the most politically progressive film imaginable, and *Flower Drum Song* hopelessly retrograde on the question of race, our discussions of film technique led them to revisit these impressions, and to write analyses that contributed to my own sense of the racial politics of both films.

---

[6] Anne Cheng, *The Melancholy of Race: Psychoanalysis, Assimilation, and Hidden Grief* (Oxford: Oxford University Press, 2000). Teachers might also point to the importance of this context by prefacing *Flower Drum Song* with a short documentary on DVD entitled *The Slanted Screen* (dir. Jeff Adachi, 2007) which concerns the gendering of Asian male actors in Hollywood cinema.

# The Use of Spike Lee's **Bamboozled** to Promote *Difficult Dialogues on Race*

**Stephen E. Slaner & Sandra Clyne**

*Northern Essex Community College &
Northeastern University/Bunker Hill Community College*

─────────────

sslaner@necc.mass.edu • sandraclyne@hotmail.com

**Abstract:** This paper will explore pedagogical strategies for using Spike Lee's cinematic coup *Bamboozled* to stimulate thoughtful discourse about race in the college classroom. The combined use of film excerpts, writing exercises and classroom discussion can help students to deconstruct racial stereotyping in the media. The students are asked initially not to converse about their emotional reactions to excerpts from the film, but to write about these responses for a brief ten to fifteen minute period. Having loosened up the flow of ideas through *freewriting*, the students are now ready to engage in a classroom discussion of the film clip. This oral discourse is followed by another, more reflective bout of writing, affording the students an opportunity to consolidate their ideas. Since *Bamboozled* portrays black performers in blackface in a "New Millennium Minstrel Show," it displays virtually every imaginable stereotype about African-Americans. The film *denaturalizes* the racial stereotypes it depicts by making them the focus of our explicit attention and by showing us their historical origins. Like Kurosawa's *Rashomon,* the film's narrative is built through interweaving the discontinuities among multiple perspectives. So the viewer must become an active participant in the effort to untangle the film's meaning as well as a catalyst for understanding and deconstructing the racial stereotypes. *Bamboozled* is an ideal candidate for Paulo Freire's strategy of *conscientization,* since it can be used as a codification that facilitates students in actively coming to grips with contemporary American racism.

This paper, which is the outgrowth of a presentation at UMass Boston's Center for the Improvement of Teaching (CIT) Annual Conference on Teaching for Transformation held in 2008, will explore pedagogical strategies for using feature films to stimulate

Stephen E. Slaner, Ed.D., is a member of the full-time faculty in government at Northern Essex Community College, where he teaches Introduction to Political Science, American Government and Politics, and History and Film. He also teaches at Northeastern's College of Professional Studies and at Bunker Hill Community College. He earned an M.Phil. in political science at Columbia University, an M.Ed. in counseling at Northeastern University, and an Ed.D. in Learning and Teaching at Harvard University. Mr. Slaner has had a lifetime of participation in movements for peace and social justice. Sandra Clyne, M.A., Psy.D., is a part-time lecturer in English at Northeastern University and a member of the adjunct faculty in psychology at Bunker Hill Community College. Her fine art photography has been shown in a variety of community and academic settings. She earned an M.A. in applied linguistics at the University of Massachusetts Boston and a Psy.D. at the Massachusetts School of Professional Psychology. Ms. Clyne is particularly interested in creativity and the development of creative process.

thoughtful discourse about race in the college classroom. We have selected Spike Lee's cinematic coup *Bamboozled* as the focus of this paper because of its frontal assault on the use of racial stereotypes in the communications media.[1]

Experience has shown us that a teacher's attempts to kindle discussion about difficult sociopolitical issues often result in students going into "silent mode." Alternatively, a bedlam can erupt in which everyone's talking and no one's listening. The combined use of film excerpts, writing exercises and classroom discussion can help students to thoughtfully develop and express their responses to complex issues about race in American society.

Feature films that deal with racial issues tend to make use of racial stereotyping in two basic ways: (1) the deconstruction of racial stereotypes and (2) the exploitation of racial stereotypes for their entertainment value. Spike Lee's *Bamboozled* is an intricate blend of both. The film has a clever story line. An African-American television writer, Pierre Delacroix (referred to as "De La"), pilots a minstrel show for the new millennium, replete with such "three dimensional" blackface characters as *Man Tan, Sleep 'n' Eat,* and *Aunt Jemima.* De La's initial intention was to excite popular outrage so that he could get himself fired from the station and thus be rid of a job he is tired of. To De La's surprise, however, the show becomes a huge success and the popular outcry against it is largely ignored. De La and the African-American entertainers he's recruited from the street, Manray and Womack, thus become twenty-first century promulgators of the crassest form of racial stereotyping of American blacks as lazy, ignorant, self-effacing buffoons. The film

ends violently with explosions of rage directed towards De La and his key performer, the talented tap dancer dubbed *Man Tan.*

Cynthia Lucia's analysis of the film poses two probing questions: "To what degree do viewers participate in the very processes they are positioned by the film to criticize? And to what degree does the film, itself, participate in the very processes it seeks to expose?"[2] On the one hand, the film *educates* the viewer about the very explicit derogatory stereotypes of African-Americans initiated during the era of the minstrel shows (mid-19th and to early 20th century) and sustained, as Spike Lee pointed out at a recent talk at Northeastern University, until the present day.[3] The story line requires that the newly recruited street performers be made to *understand* the motifs of the minstrel era, and so De La and his sleek assistant Sloane instruct them while simultaneously deepening their own understanding of the genre. We see documentary footage of tap dancers from the Deep South, vintage footage of *Amos 'n' Andy,* and animated cartoons, as well as numerous dolls and figurines that display the shiny black faces, wide eyes and red lips of the comical stereotype of the African-American. Likewise, Lee shows us the complex emotional responses of the performers who must "black up" before going on stage. On the other hand, Lee creates a highly *entertaining* pageant of traditional minstrel show entertainment. So the students viewing excerpts from the film must sort out a maze of apparently contradictory signals about racial stereotyping.

Our strategy is to begin the classroom exercise by showing the archival footage at the film's conclusion, an excerpt of about three and a half minutes. As De La lies ex-

---

[1] The presentation also discussed Warren Beatty's film *Bulworth* (1998), but space limitations make it necessary to focus only on *Bamboozled.* Those interested in using *Bulworth* may contact the lead author at sslaner@necc.mass.edu for helpful suggestions.

[2] Cynthia Lucia, "Race, Media and Money: A Critical Symposium on Spike Lee's *Bamboozled.*" *Cineaste,* Vol. XXVI, No. 2, p. 11.
[3] March 21, 2008, Blackman Auditorium, Northeastern University, Boston.

sanguinating on the floor of his luxury condo, the audience is treated to the pastiche of traditional racial stereotypes he has been viewing on his VCR: movie cartoons from the first half of the twentieth century, excerpts of racist feature films like *Birth of a Nation* and *The Jazz Singer*, documentary footage of soft shoe and tap from the era of the advent of film, newsreels of watermelon-eating contests, and the like. The stereotypical content includes visual exaggerations of facial and bodily characteristics: shiny black faces, huge, "liver" lips, bulging white eyes, rotund women with skinny, diminutive men, and of course, *blackface* makeup for both blacks and whites. Personality characterizations include vacant stares, slow, slurred speech, exaggerated deference to whites, fearful trembling, spasmodic gesturing, cannibalism, and gustatory excitements occasioned by chicken houses and "nigger apples."

The students' first reactions to the film clip might range from bewilderment to outraged indignation to outright amusement. The students are asked initially not to discuss these responses, but to write about them for a brief ten to fifteen minute period. This strategy, suggested at the CIT conference by Dr. Vivian Zamel of UMass Boston, would allow the students to develop and express their emotional and conceptual responses to the onslaught of raw, crass racial stereotyping. Having loosened up the flow of ideas through *freewriting*, the students are now ready to engage in a classroom discussion of the film clip. The writing exercise will have served to modulate the students' tendency to "clam up" into a self-conscious silence or, alternatively, to gush forth with a stream of careless remarks. The classroom discussion is followed by another, more reflective bout of writing, affording the students an opportunity to consolidate their ideas. The structure of this writing exercise reflects Peter Elbow's observation:

Writing calls on two skills that are so different that they usually conflict with each other: creating and criticizing.... Most of the time it helps to separate the creating and criticizing processes so they don't interfere with each other: first write freely and uncritically so that you can generate as many words and ideas as possible without worrying whether they are good; then turn around and adopt a critical frame of mind and thoroughly revise what you have written—taking what's good and discarding what isn't and shaping what's left into something strong. [Elbow (1981), p. 7.]

This two-step process of unfettered *freewriting* followed by thoughtful revision is here utilized to promote the difficult dialogue about racial stereotyping in the media.

In the next phase of discourse about the film, the students are asked a *scaffolding* question: To what extent do racial stereotypes in the media influence our self-concepts and behavior? After posing the question, the teacher shows a brief clip from the film that displays the conflicted emotional responses of the black performers when they "black up" before going on stage. Spike Lee contrasts their reactions by showing more resentment, anger, and humiliation on the part of Sleep'n'Eat and more resignation on the part of Mantan, and also by using softer colors (brown and red) for Sleep'n'Eat and harsher colors (green and black) for Mantan. Their ambivalence is shown by rear shots of each character along with *two separate reflections* in the mirror, as if embodying W. E. B. Du Bois' famous concept of "two souls," one reflecting the way black folks see themselves and the other the way they are seen by whites. The minstrel show, of course, expresses the white half of the split. Indeed, Spike Lee's commentary on the DVD points out that Tommy Davidson, the actor who plays Sleep'n'Eat, has a moment of insight as he applies the finishing touches to his black-face and cries "real tears." It is interesting to note that despite his facial expression of disgust and humiliation backstage, Sleep'n'Eat assumes the stereotypical role of the dumb Negro on stage, while Man Tan, who seemed less conflicted to begin with, is positively gleeful and very much into the part. In this rapidly edited scene, Spike Lee conveys a range of emotional dynamics that makes the viewer viscerally aware of the devastating psychological impact of accepting the demeaning role assigned to black entertainers by their white bosses.

At this point, we will turn our attention to a critical analysis of *Bamboozled* that will further clarify our rationale for selecting this film as a stimulus for classroom discussion about race and racial stereotypes. We can view *Bamboozled* through the lens of another film, Cuban director T.G. Alea's *The Last Supper* (1976). Here a 19th-century slave revolt is portrayed as the outcome of the glaring contradiction between the masters' rhetoric of equality before God and the slaves' condition of gross inequality and subordination. In the course of an Easter dinner, one of the slaves relates the following parable from his own culture:

> When Olofi made the world, he made it complete: he made the day, he made the night; he made good things, he made bad things; he also made lovely things and … ugly things…. He made Truth and also he made the Lie. The Truth appeared nice to him. The Lie did not seem good to him: it was ugly and skinny … as if it were sick. Olofi thinks it pitiful and gives it a sharp machete to defend itself. Time passed and people always wanted to go with the Truth, but no one, no one wanted to go with the Lie. One day Truth and the Lie met each other in the road and as they

are enemies they fight. Truth is stronger than the Lie, but the Lie has the sharp machete which Olofi gave him. When Truth was careless and dropped his guard, the Lie—zip!—cut off Truth's head. Truth no longer has eyes and begins to look for his head with his hands. Looking and looking he suddenly blunders into the head of the Lie and—whup!—pulls off the Lie's head and puts it where his own had been. *And from then on he goes about the world, deceiving all the people, the body of Truth with the head of the Lie.* [Cited in Downing (1987), pp. 292-293; emphasis added.]

This parable is an ingenious answer to the New Testament stories recounted by the plantation owner, whose message of love and equality is belied by the obvious fact that the Africans have no rights, are not treated as human beings, and are anything but equal in Cuban society. The Truth in Jesus' message, of course, is that the slaves *should* be treated as free and equal human beings, but then they would not be slaves: Truth with the head of the Lie.

Next we shall examine how *Bamboozled* deconstructs historical images of African-Americans in a very different way from *The Last Supper*, but still with the idea of unmasking Truth with the head of the Lie. We will close with some observations by renowned education theorist Paulo Freire about the use of *codification* as a means of stimulating critical reflection.

*Bamboozled* builds on Melvin Van Peebles' *Classified X* (1998) in exposing the way in which African-Americans have historically been portrayed in American cinema.[4] The montage of actual images at the end of *Bamboozled* that we discussed earlier serves as a documentary counterpoint to the fierce satire we have seen up to that point. Before analyzing the film, we would like to situate it in terms of the images of Africa that precede the emergence of cinema by centuries.

In his authoritative work *White on Black* (1992), Jan Pieterse amply demonstrates that race is a social construction, since the stereotypes of blacks in European and American culture clearly reflect the perceptions of whites—in turn related to their position of domination with respect to Africa—rather than the realities at the time. This stereotyping did not cease with the end of slavery; in fact, according to Pieterse (1992, pp. 57, 63),

> The period of abolitionism coincided with the rise of racism. The humanization of the image of blacks in abolitionist propaganda went hand in hand with the hardening of that image through the application of the category "race." … Race established new social boundaries at the very time the old ones were annulled.

A new imperialism emerged that replaced the image of the "noble savage," itself a European distortion, with that of the "ignoble savage." Now the Europeans would take up "the White Man's burden," in Kipling's famous phrase, to tame the "savages" they encountered. Then, as noted by Pieterse (1992, pp. 88-89),

> A new mythology of Africa took shape which met the needs of established colonialism. Savages had to be turned into political subjects. … Colonial paternalism engendered as its counterpart the infantilism of the colonized.

Whether seen as savages or children, Africans were obviously not perceived to be on the same plane as "civilized" Europeans. Similarly, even if they were no longer actually slaves, people of African descent in the New World were not accorded the same status as whites. (Indeed certain ethnic groups, most notably Jews and Irish, had to *become* white, and stereotyping of these groups was quite common through the early 20th century.[5])

So the stereotypes continued and came to be reflected in the emerging U.S. entertainment industry—which is where *Bamboozled* comes in. As discussed above, in suggesting that his network put on a *New Millennium Minstrel Show*, in which black performers would be wearing blackface, TV writer Pierre Delacroix at first wants to devise a show so outrageous that its failure is assured[6] and he will therefore be released from his contract. As a black writer in a white-dominated industry, he feels with some justification that his views are not taken seriously by his boss, Thomas Dunwitty. Spike Lee's camera placement reinforces this idea, since at the meeting of network writers we look *down* on De La and *up* to Dunwitty. It is quite clear who has the power in this situation. Just as in *The Last Supper*, advantaged whites are inviting blacks to the table, but the terms are prearranged and lead to destruction and violence in both cases.

To De La's surprise, Dunwitty goes for the minstrel show. Indeed, it is evident that he seems himself as someone who really understands blacks, partly because (as he

---

[4] Spike Lee acknowledges his debt to this documentary in Crowdus and Georgakas (2001, p. 4): "I was amazed by the imagery, so I contacted the film's researcher … since she'd done a lot of the work already, and she was able to get us a lot of this material…. None of us had seen this material. For example, I had never seen Bugs Bunny in blackface!"

[5] This again reinforces the point that it is a question not of skin color, since these groups "look" white, but of social construction.
[6] This is similar to Mel Brooks' 1968 film *The Producers*, in which the protagonists put on a play, "Springtime for Hitler," in the hope that it will be a total failure so that their insurance policy will pay off. To their amazement, the play is a smash hit. (In the DVD commentary, Spike Lee acknowledges his debt to this film and to Budd Schulberg's *The Face in the Crowd*, a 1957 media exposé.)

says) he is married to a black woman. So whereas De La has a distinctively "white" accent, Dunwitty sounds "black." Recalling the metaphor from *The Last Supper*, the Truth of De La's whiteness and Dunwitty's blackness comes with the head of the Lie, in at least two senses: (1) Despite De La's affectations and desire to succeed in a white world, he is in fact black, just as Dunwitty is definitely white; *and* (2) De La's blackness and Dunwitty's whiteness are themselves social creations and therefore a kind of illusion (or collective delusion, if you will). In any event, Dunwitty adopts the minstrel show idea as his own and makes it even more degrading, if possible, than De La had intended, as the stereotypes come to embrace not only the performers but the audience as well. The underlying truth here is captured by Spike Lee (Crowdus and Georgakas, 2001, p. 5):

> Culture should be appreciated by everybody, but for me there is a distinction between *appreciation* of a culture and *appropriation* of a culture. People like Dunwitty are dangerous because they appropriate black culture and put a spin on it as if they are the originators of it. There's a big difference.

Note that this distinction is reinforced by the different ways the minstrel show and the film itself are shot. As Davis points out (2002, p. 17):

> Lee and Kuras [his cinematographer] made the esthetic choice to shoot on digital cameras those scenes involving the characters interacting in their daily lives, while the scenes involving *The New Millennium Minstrel Show* were shot on the more richly detailed Super 16 camera.

To put it another way, the minstrel show is going to be "larger than life," just as the impact of black stereotypes throughout American media and culture has been to transform daily life itself, making it stylized in a particularly destructive way.

In this context, it is important to remember how the minstrel show originated historically:

> One of the first black figures to achieve popularity in modern western culture was the Minstrel— a white imitation of black culture. Or, more accurately, in the words of Kenneth Lynn, "a white imitation of a black imitation of a contented slave." [Pieterse, 1992, p. 132.]

So whites were imitating blacks imitating the white image of blacks.[7]

Moreover, the response to these stereotypes—deliberately shown in an over-the-top way—is itself stereotyped, in at least two ways. First, the phenomenon of *internalizing the aggressor* is shown in De La's willingness to go along with the minstrel show despite (because of?) its cruel and destructive nature. This is graphically shown in the reactions of the two dancers in the minstrel show, Mantan and Sleep'n'Eat. A similar phenomenon was seen in concentration camps where some Jewish inmates were assigned the role of kapo to police their fellow inmates for the Nazis. Second, the resistance to black acquiescence in white domination is shown by the Mau Maus, who execute Mantan on television. In a way, this conforms to the image of blacks as violent, aggressive, even gangsters,[8] not a group that has a clear and coherent alternative to the powers-that-be.

The critical reaction to *Bamboozled* was mixed. Some commentators seemed to

---

[7] This wheel-within-wheels phenomenon is used in a different way by Blake Edwards in *Victor Victoria* (1982) to show sexual stereotyping, as Julie Andrews is cast in the role of a woman imitating a man imitating a woman.

lump the film together with that which it was attacking. Noted black film critic Armond White, for example, declared that

> ... Lee is his own work of art, an example of social and professional ascension, exemplifying personal foible and contradiction.... By confusing issues of showbiz representation and career ethics through his inherent inconsistency and apoplexy, Lee's films hinder and exacerbate rather than clarify. [White, 2001, p. 13.]

White comes perilously close to arguing that since Spike Lee has "made it"—that is, since his films have mass-market distribution and he has celebrity cachet—the impact of the stereotypes he criticizes is not so great as to prevent the emergence of directors who challenge those very stereotypes. The argument is ingenious, and reminiscent of bygone days when it was argued that the fact that Jackie Robinson broke into the major leagues with the Brooklyn Dodgers "proved" that racism in sports was either nonexistent or not as bad as people thought. Of course it proved nothing of the kind. Racism was a real problem in sports (and still is in terms of who controls the various teams), and it remains a real problem in American media and culture, notwithstanding the success of Spike Lee and other independent black filmmakers. Spike Lee is not saying that racist stereotyping is anywhere and everywhere all-powerful, but it *is* a huge force in American life whose impact we ignore at our peril.

The real point of *Bamboozled*, in fact, is to *denaturalize* those stereotypes by calling attention to them and showing how they were historically constructed. As we dis-

cussed earlier, one of the most powerful scenes in the movie involves the two main characters putting on blackface. We get to see how the blackface was prepared and the psychological impact it has on those who have to wear it. Art and reality are combined in this scene, since the idea of black people wearing blackface happened only in a Spike Lee movie, but *metaphorically* many blacks have been wearing blackface insofar as they conform to the image that white people have of them. This might be seen as the Lie with the head of Truth, since the literal improbability of the image is much less significant than the deeper underlying reality that Spike Lee is getting at.

There is a larger issue here as well. In a recent paper on the work of French film theorist Gilles Deleuze, Amy Herzog (2005) raises the question of "how we might think about cinematic spectacles in relation to the notion of a historical image" (p. 2). *Bamboozled*, of course, is a spectacle that is trying to position itself in relation to actual images—some of which we see at the end—of the black experience. As Spike Lee's film is a spectacle which is in part a musical, Herzog's comments may apply to it:

> In the musical, the dance is our dream, and the movement between dream-world and "reality" is, to greater or lesser degrees, open and ambiguous. The significance of the musical number rests in its rupturing of the sensory-motor situations that define the movement-image. [2005, p. 6.]

The *dream-image*, Herzog goes on to argue, is part of what Foucault calls

> ...a new means of perceiving and conceptualizing, a "historical sense" that counters the pillars of Platonic history (reality, identity, and truth) with parody, dissociation, and the powers of the false. [2005, p. 8.]

---

⁸ Spike Lee says in the DVD commentary that gangsta rap is a kind of stereotype that doesn't advance the interests of blacks. He reiterated this position at his recent talk at Northeastern.

"Parody ... and the powers of the false" are certainly evident throughout *Bamboozled*, which is nothing if not parody. Moreover, the film is like a dream in that inanimate objects take on a life of their own (the Jolly Nigger Bank), the dead speak (De La, the narrator, has been killed by his assistant Sloan), and the minstrel show itself is nightmarish. Now consider Herzog's point about the potentialities of cinema:

> [For Deleuze] the cinema is a creative process that can act to excavate, to provoke, to make the previously imperceptible perceptible. Engagement with the cinema becomes a means of generating new thought, of rethinking history. The question is how to understand the modality by which a film operates. Does the film ... build its narrative through chronological progressions or through discontinuities and chance? Is identity asserted as a unified whole, or is it dissociated, contradictory, and multiple? Does the film aspire to speak the truth, or does it wage a battle against universals through fiction and fabulation? [2005, p. 8.]

In terms of *Bamboozled*, the narrative is built primarily through discontinuities among multiple perspectives—as in Kurosawa's celebrated film *Rashomon*—and the viewer must be an active participant in the effort to untangle the film's meaning. Identity is definitely "dissociated, contradictory, and multiple," as we discussed earlier with respect to De La and Dunwitty's positioning themselves on the black/white continuum. As to the last point, the film is aspiring to speak a larger truth, but it does so precisely through fiction and fabulation. Thus *Bamboozled* transcends the antinomies put forward by Herzog: it is not "either/ or" but "both/and" for some of her questions. Finally, there is no question that

"generating new thought" and "rethinking history" are goals of the film, whose purpose is to shake things up and open up new avenues of discourse. We must repeat that the notion of Truth with the head of the Lie is key to the film, along with the idea that the task of all of us—film director, actor, and viewer alike—is to change the reality it so eloquently criticizes. Before we can change it, however, we must understand it, and that means confronting unpleasant realities about American media and culture. In this sense the ultimate target of *Bamboozled* is not, or not only, racial stereotypes: "The driving force of Lee's story," Landau argues (2002, p. 12), "is contemporary, untamed capitalism in its mad race for profits or, in media jargon, ratings." In other words, we are talking not only about *race* but also about *class*.[9]

If there are still masters—and there most certainly are—they reside in a new kind of plantation, the corporation, and its handmaidens in politics. The slaves are no longer picking cotton; in fact, they are not legally slaves. In terms of who has power in society, however, the master-slave dichotomy is still applicable. The irony is that on *this* plantation the slaves can, if they wish, rebel. It is therefore the task of the media, among other institutions, to make sure that that thought never crosses their minds.[10] And here is where Spike Lee's movie really has something to teach us: just as the media are busy promoting racial stereotypes, so they replace real news with manufactured

---

[9] In this connection, Pieterse (1992, p. 51) notes that "the key notion underlying [racist] discourses is not so much that of race as of *hierarchy* based on differences in religion, ethnicity, geography, nationality, culture, or a combination of these." Class, of course, is a persistent and powerful form of hierarchy. Landau argues (2001, p. 12), and we agree, that "Lee has done in one film more to enlighten audiences on race, class, history and entertainment than Hollywood has done in a century."

[10] On this point see, among others, Chomsky and Herman (1988). For the philosophical implications, see especially Marcuse (1964).

reality in which the slaves, if slaves they are, acquiesce in their own slavery. The discomfort many critics feel at seeing *Bamboozled* is really the discomfort we all feel at living in an artificial reality that masquerades as the real thing: Truth with the head of the Lie.

## CONCLUSION

Renowned Brazilian educator Paulo Freire initiated the use of a visual "code" or codification—which can include photographs or films—to stimulate critical thinking among students:

> In my case, the codification works as a challenge, a challenge to the students and the educator…. The codification is an object to be known, and to the extent that codification represents a part of the concrete reality, in trying to understand or to describe the codification, you are again trying to understand the concrete reality in which you are. (Freire & Horton, 1990, pp. 87-89)

Mayo summarizes the opportunities made possible by this use of codification:

> Codifications can … be used not simply to facilitate processes whereby the present is viewed critically, to obtain greater awareness of the contradictions underlying it, but also as a means of engendering the dialectical process, involving the juxtaposition of and critical reflection upon past and present. This dialectical process can open up possibilities for transformation. (Mayo, 1999, p. 148)

*Bamboozled* can function as a codification in Freire's sense to enable students to see and understand the racial stereotypes

in our culture that too often go unseen. While it is true that the grossest traditional racial stereotypes have been superseded by more subtle ones in today's media, the stigma of racial inferiority that such stereotyping engenders is still present. The real danger is in the lack of a proper historical context for our discourse about race, a deficit that Spike Lee's *Bamboozled* strives to remediate. It is the legacy of slavery that is simultaneously portrayed and deconstructed by Spike Lee, and for that reason alone *Bamboozled* deserves serious consideration in any pedagogical strategy to expose students to the minefield that is race in America in 2008.

BIBLIOGRAPHY

Alea, T.G. (1976). *The Last Supper.* New Yorker Video.

Beatty, W. (1998). *Bulworth.* 20th-Century Fox.

Brooks, M. (1968). *The Producers.* MGM.

Chomsky, N. and Herman, E. (1988). *Manufacturing Consent.* New York: Pantheon Books.

Crowdus, G. and Georgakas, D. (2001). "Thinking About the Power of Images: An Interview with Spike Lee." *Cineaste,* Vol. XXVI, No. 2, pp. 4-9.

Davis, Z. (2001). "'Beautiful-Ugly' Blackface: An Esthetic Appreciation of *Bamboozled.*" *Cineaste,* Vol. XXVI, No. 2, pp. 16-17.

Downing, J.D.H. (1987). *Film and Politics in the Third World.* New York: Autonomedia.

Edwards, B. (1992). *Victor Victoria.* MGM.

Elbow, P. (1981). *Writing with Power.* New York: Oxford University Press.

Freire, P. and Horton, M. (1990). *We Make the Road by Walking.* Philadelphia: Temple University Press.

Herzog, A. (2005). "Becoming-Fluid: History, Corporeality, and the Musical Spectacle." Paper delivered at conference on Gilles Deleuze, Carpenter Center for the Visual Arts, Harvard University.

Landau, S. (2001). "Spike Lee's Revolutionary Broadside." *Cineaste,* Vol. XXVI, No. 2, pp. 11-12.

Lee, S. (2000). *Bamboozled.* New Line Cinema.

Lucia, C. (2001). "Race, Media and Money: A Critical Symposium on Spike Lee's *Bamboozled*" *Cineaste*, Vol. XXVI, No. 2, p. 11.

Marcuse, H. (1964). *One-Dimensional Man*. Boston: Beacon Press.

Mayo, P. (1999). *Gramsci, Freire and Adult Education: Possibilities for Transformative Action*. London: Zed Books.

Pieterse, J.N. (1992). *White on Black: Images of Africa and Blacks in Western Popular Culture*. New Haven: Yale University Press.

Rogin, M. (2001). "Nowhere Left to Stand: The Burnt Cork Roots of Popular Culture." *Cineaste*, Vol. XXVI, No. 2, pp. 14-15.

Schulberg, B. (1957). *A Face in the Crowd*. Warner Bros.

Tate, G. (2001). "*Bamboozled*: White Supremacy and a Black Way of Being Human," *Cineaste*, Vol. XXVI, No. 2, pp. 15-16.

Van Peebles, M. (1998). *Classified X*. Fox Lorber.

White, A. (2001). "Post-Art Minstrelsy." *Cineaste*, Vol. XXVI, No. 2, pp. 12-14.

# Making Assessment Everyone's Business

## The Use of Dialogue in Improving Teaching and Learning

### John Chetro-Szivos & Lauren Mackenzie

*Fitchburg State College*

————————————————

jchetro@fsc.edu • lmacken4@fsc.edu

**Abstract:** In the 2007/2008 academic year, five faculty in the Department of Communication Media at Fitchburg State College came together to seek ways to be proactive in addressing the challenges imposed by outcomes assessment. The goal of this study was to see if opportunities existed to find constructive ways to engage assessment beyond the positions of those who are opposed or cautious about it. This article introduces a communication perspective for studying assessment; provides a detailed overview of the components of the study; discusses the findings and connects them to a systemic approach for looking at assessment; and concludes by emphasizing the importance of synthesizing assessment, dialogue, and self-reflection.

## INTRODUCTION

There is little doubt that outcomes assessment has become the cornerstone of the accreditation process. Regional accreditation bodies regard outcomes assessment as vital to measuring the effectiveness of institutions of higher education and require institutions to develop outcomes assessment plans. In the current climate there are faculty and administrators who wholly support assessment and those who are vehemently opposed, with many falling somewhere in between these positions and cautiously observing the movement towards assessment.[1] In spite of the opposition and caution, assessment is a reality and part of the life of the academy. This is evident as external bodies, including the federal government, routinely ask to what degree students reach the goals of an established curriculum.

Our goal in the conduct of this study was to see if opportunities existed to find constructive ways to engage assessment beyond the positions of those who are opposed or cautious about assessment. We designed the study so that faculty could experience and explore the challenges of the outcomes assessment and its effect on

————————————————

[1] It should be noted that the New England region differs somewhat from other regional accreditation associations. The New England Association has been less directive in terms of outcomes assessment than what occurred in other parts of the country.

————————————————

John Chetro-Szivos is Associate Professor and Chair of the Department of Media Communications at Fitchburg State College. His interests include human interaction in a wide variety of setting most notably intercultural encounters, artistic dimensions of experience, conversational spaces in educational and organizational settings, cross-gender issues, and building dialogue for civic transformation. Lauren Mackenzie is Assistant Professor at the Department of Media Communication at Fitchburg State College. Her research interests include ethnography of communication, interpersonal communication theory, and community service learning.

teaching and learning in our classes and ultimately our department.

We brought together five faculty in our Department of Communication Media to seek ways to be proactive in addressing the challenges imposed by outcomes assessment. During the Fall 2007 semester, these five faculty experimented with the development of assessment outcomes for one assignment in one of their courses. The courses ranged from introductory communication theory to advanced communication theory courses and included two courses in film production. Each faculty member selected one assignment and developed a rubric according to guiding principles that would assess what students learned. The rubric served as a guide to evaluate the students' work. In the study, rubrics served as an instrument to assist the faculty in measuring student work as clearly and consistently as possible by defining the criteria to judge and measure performance. Although this was not a study in rubrics, we found them helpful as a means to organize and interpret data gathered from observations of student learning.

The faculty met several times throughout the semester and participated in discussions about rubrics, teaching, learning, and the assessment process. After the assignments were completed, the faculty held a discussion about the effectiveness of all aspects of the project. This study provided the faculty with an opportunity to reflect and learn about ways to approach the assessment challenge.

In completing the study we certainly became aware of the challenges of assessment and soon discovered the opportunities it provided for a group of scholars. We recognized that the strengths of the assessment process lay in the kind of critical inquiry and thoughtful self-reflection we were able to engage in as a result of our discussions.

The remainder of this article will be or-

ganized as follows: first, we introduce a communication perspective for studying assessment; second, we give a detailed overview of the various components of the study; next, we discuss our findings and connect them to a systemic approach for looking at assessment; finally, we conclude by emphasizing the importance of synthesizing assessment, dialogue, and self-reflection.

## A COMMUNICATION PERSPECTIVE

Our work is grounded in what has been called the communication perspective (Pearce, 1989). Briefly, the communication perspective contends that communication is more than a simple process to express our inner thoughts or a way of describing objects and events in the world. Instead it recognizes communication as the primary social process—meaning, it is the way that we create, sustain, and change our understanding of all things. We come to know things in our world through the process of communication; this includes persons, relations, and institutions. The communication perspective argues that communication is necessary for human association, and our lives become the sum total of conversations and exchanges with others. We achieve understanding, or a like-mindedness, when we have the ability to act with others and share the meaning of objects, events, and actions (Chetro-Szivos, 2006).

In this study, the dialogue between faculty served as the key element in coming to understand the assessment process and co-construct ways that assessment could enhance teaching and learning. We intentionally designed the study so that the faculty had ample opportunity to exchange ideas by meeting face-to-face and sharing numerous emails and postings about the project. Communication was not reduced to mere epiphenomena, it became the basis for building new understandings and shared knowledge of how assessment could contribute to the improvement of our teaching and learning practices.

Given the focus on communication, we found the strength of the study lay in the ability to use dialogue to think about the challenges of teaching and learning. Our inquiry was centered on several guiding questions. We asked:

1. In what ways can faculty learn to use the assessment process to think and act systemically so they may enhance their teaching and learning?
2. When faculty engage in dialogue about teaching and learning, what impact can it have on helping students attain the stated outcomes of a curriculum?
3. What improvements come about in teaching and learning through the dialogic process?
4. In what ways do rubrics enhance or limit teaching, learning, or measuring student performance and what alternatives exist aside from rubrics that can help us assess student learning?

## THE STUDY

As stated above, the study included five faculty who each selected one assignment and developed a rubric to assess their students' work. The participating faculty included four junior faculty at the assistant professor level and one tenured faculty member at the associate level. This was the first semester of full time teaching for two of the assistant professors and the other two assistant professors were in their second year of full-time teaching. Prior to coming to our college on a tenure track, all had extensive records of teaching as adjuncts or on temporary appointment. The remaining faculty member was in his eighth year of full-time teaching. The faculty met over a ten-week period during the semester. The first meeting was used to de-

scribe the study and explain the rubric template for assessing students' work. The rubrics were designed as a template but each faculty member selected the elements of the assignment used to grade the degree of the students' demonstrated competency. What was consistent across the rubrics was the use of a four-point scale with a score of one being equivalent to beginning level of performance; two indicated that the student was developing and moving towards mastery; a score of three meant that the student was reflecting mastery; and a student could earn a score of four as an indication of the highest level of performance (see the Appendix).

In our first meeting we invited faculty to feel free to express their opinions on outcomes assessment, rubrics, and grading. The faculty did talk about their skepticism and fear about outcomes assessment. Generally, faculty saw assessment as a threat to academic freedom and in conflict with their pedagogical beliefs. Most of the faculty felt that rubrics presented limitations as a reliable or valid measure of student performance. However, all faculty agreed to enter into the assessment process and remain open in evaluating its effectiveness.

At the second meeting, the faculty reported on the positive and negative aspects of the assignment they selected and the rubric used to evaluate it. This was a lively discussion about teaching, learning, and assessing students' work. Faculty exchanged many ideas and resources about approaches to teaching, learning, and assessment. The faculty found that in the process of identifying and articulating the expected outcomes of the assignment they clarified the purpose of the assignment (which also made the faculty verify that they were consistent with overall course goals) and were able to give students more direction and feedback on their performance.

Some of the faculty expressed concerns about the validity of measurement, asking how could they be certain that their rubric was measuring the students' knowledge. This became a pressing issue for the two faculty teaching film production courses. The film courses included a scriptwriting course that required students to prepare a storyboard and a lighting course where students were asked to light a set. These two faculty expressed concerns about grading creative work against established standards. Their primary concern was that standards might limit the students' choices in completing the assignment. They felt students could find other ways of completing the assignment that were highly creative, but outside of the boundaries of the rubric. The three remaining faculty teaching communication theory courses did not express such concerns about grading the ability to think critically or thinking in original ways. It is worth noting that this may in part be attributed to the difference in the educational preparation of the faculty. The two film faculty were educated in art schools, both earning Master of Fine Arts degrees, while the three theorists earned Doctor of Philosophy degrees in communication. Their respective fields may place values on different aspects of student and work and perhaps there are pedagogical differences between the two fields.

Overall, the faculty agreed that the experience was helpful and provided them with new insights into teaching, learning, and assessment. They stated that they enjoyed the meetings and the opportunity the meetings offered to reflect on their teaching. Prior to the third meeting, we asked the faculty to write a one-page reflective summary of the process and their participation in the study. They were asked to identify the strengths and weaknesses of the project and share thoughts they had about the experience. We analyzed their summaries and identified the major themes in the faculties' writing. The findings were categorized into five areas and given to the faculty to review before the third meeting. The faculty identified the following insights and concerns in the five areas listed below:

1.  Clarity – defining the outcomes created greater accountability and provided students with an explanation of the grading process and the requirements of the assignment. This helped faculty to be more clear with students about expectations of the assignment and its purpose in the course. Overall, they felt this study led them to constructively question what they do and how they can do it better.

2.  Dialogue – the dialogue between the faculty was regarded as reassuring and deepened a sense of belonging to the department. The faculty pointed to this exercise as effective in encouraging collaboration and providing an opportunity to reflect together on teaching and learning. Faculty stated that they learned more about teaching and learning through these sessions than other events they had participated in on campus. They felt the dialogue created a sense of working together and made them feel more positively connected to the department. Through these discussions they could see positive aspects of outcomes assessment and ways it could strengthen teaching, learning, and the institution.

3.  Overlap – faculty felt they could better understand the overlap between what is taught in production courses and what is taught in theory courses giving them a better sense of their part in the curriculum and the students' education at our college. This helped faculty to think of ways to help the students make connections among the courses they take in the department and the importance of faculty learning about what their colleagues do.

4.  Resources – the discussions encouraged faculty to share a number of resources such as books and journal

articles that they found helpful in learning about assessment. Faculty found that the dialogues introduced them to a wider variety of resources than they would have found on their own.

5. Rubrics – faculty found that the rubrics both reduced the time spent in grading and worked as an effective instrument for evaluating most assignments. The faculty agreed that the act of identifying the criteria for evaluation helped them to think critically about the relationship of the assignment to the course objectives. It also refined their ideas and expectations for competencies the students should be developing through the assignment and in the course. Some faculty did not share the rubric prior to the grading of the assignment and those faculty decided that in the future they would review the rubric with the students prior to the assignment due date. The use of the rubric allowed the faculty to question how they teach and assess creative work as well as critical thinking.

At the third meeting the faculty discussed the five areas listed above and came to consensus that the process was valuable in teaching them about their own teaching. In addition, the faculty talked about how important it was to work together on issues that they all faced, and how what they taught was related to the other faculty in the department. Most of the participants reported that approaching assessment in this format made them feel less anxious about the process of outcomes assessment. Faculty felt that it was important to take an active role in establishing the outcomes and measuring what the students achieved as opposed to an assessment program imposed on them from above or from an external body.

## MAKING SENSE OF THE FINDINGS

We regard the concern faculty expressed about grading and the validity of grading students' competencies as a positive feature of the project. Faculty and administrators of institutions of higher education have a responsibility to use their expertise to establish a curriculum and make sure each course and assignment contributes to meeting the goals and objective of the curriculum. Reflecting on the role of each assignment is a responsibility that should not be taken lightly. It is the role of faculty to ensure that what is done in the classroom and what is expected of students are closely related to the established purpose of a course or a curriculum. As we witnessed in the dialogues, the assessment process brought greater clarity for both the students and the faculty as they determined what was important in the course and how the assignment and their teaching relates to the intended outcomes.

We found the project provided faculty with a forum where they could express their concerns in a supportive atmosphere and receive feedback as well as discover that others share similar concerns. Their participation in the study helped to alleviate the isolation faculty may feel. A sense of isolation may come about as faculty often work independently and there is little time to share ideas about teaching and learning due to the many demands they face. Creating the time for these faculty to share their ideas about teaching and learning was a unique experience and contributed to a sense of being part of a good department. Dialogue was effective and perhaps the most important aspect of the project.

Generally speaking, dialogue is a means for two or more people to create new levels of understanding and share a common understanding. Dialogue in this instance can be called a facilitated dialogue as the faculty were presented with questions and ideas to reflect upon. Working in this way allowed the faculty to discover and gather information about teaching and learning with the purpose of promoting new ways of thinking about teaching, learning, and assessment. Consistent with Bateson's (1972) systems orientation, the faculty found ways to exceed simple cause and effect ideas about assessment and move towards a process of conjoint action that operates in a recursive manner among the faculty. Here we see evidence that communication served a far more important function than a simple exchange of ideas. Instead we saw a complex interactive process that generated, sustained, or changed the meanings of teaching, learning, and assessment for the members of the system through recursive interaction. It is clear that the faculty had a new experience with assessment and in sharing this experience it helped them to recognize the positive aspects of assessment and to work together as members of a system. Through their conversations, faculty found that assessment is not about keeping score cards on students and program performance. In this instance, assessment became a means to ask what we do with students, what happens to students in our classes, and it helped us envision how all parts of the system contribute to teaching and learning.

Thinking systemically requires that we account for all parts of the system and understand the interdependence among the parts of the system. Krippendorff (1977) indicated that systems theory emphasizes properties of wholes and parts, and relationships and hierarchies. A college or university is a complex system that is made up of many parts which includes the internal aspects such as faculty, administrators, students, curriculum, staff, and the physical plant, to name a few. There are also important aspects of the system that may be thought of as external to the institution such as accreditation bodies, prospective employers, and in the case of a public insti-

tution, the legislature. Systems theory stresses the property of wholeness, which points to the fact that the institution is a nonsummative collection of its parts. Nonsummativity refers to the notion that a college or a university is more than the sum of these parts. Together the parts create a synergy that render the entire organization greater in its capacity to function than would be recognized by simply listing the parts.

In addition to being instrumental to a successfully functioning organization, all systems exhibit the characteristic of self-regulation. Through self-regulation, the system (or in this case, the institution) makes use of feedback to set its goals and guide the actions of faculty and all members of the system. The quality of the feedback allows institutions to make better decisions and adapt to the demands of its environment. It may be argued that outcomes assessment is crucial to the institution in making decisions and setting its direction about what it provides or should provide for its students. Assessment efforts can generate information about the effectiveness of the institution's curriculum, programs, and services. As we see in the comments made by the faculty, the information they discussed and gathered through their participation in the study allowed them to think and make new connections about teaching, leaning, and the department's curriculum. Making distinctions in this way allows faculty to move closer to understanding how what they do contributes to the overall purpose of the system and how their efforts are connected to the system or the institution. It is easy to lose sight of the interdependence of the parts of an institution when days are filled with teaching classes, grading, advising, committee work, and other duties that contribute to thinking of oneself as working in isolation. Thinking systemically gives faculty the ability to understand the relationship between the parts of the department, the institution, and their role in helping the institution meet its missions and goals. We saw clear evidence of systemic thinking when the faculty recognized the overlap in their courses and how important it is to make connections to the curriculum and among their colleagues.

We found that through this project, faculty created a community that focused on their practice as educators. The impact of this association is evident in the kinds of conversations we now see among faculty. Humans are special kinds of creatures whose survival is contingent upon interacting with others and forming distinctive kinds of association called community (Cronen & Chetro-Szivos, 2001). The strength of these communities relies on the members' ability to develop appreciation for others and the interdependence they share with all parts of the community or system. These faculty dialogues became an important aspect of redefining the community and constructing new understandings about assessment and each faculty's member's role in contributing to the institution.

Angelo (2000) noted the importance of academic departments thinking and acting systemically. In his view an ideal department is one that builds a shared trust, motivation, and language. When faculty work together to construct new ways of thinking about teaching, learning, and assessment, they are meeting the components of Angelo's conception of an ideal department. They become a community that is capable of calling upon its resources to adapt to the tasks and challenges presented by academic life. The faculty who participated in the study began to make connections between the course they were teaching, their colleagues' courses, and the curriculum offered by the department. This web of interdependence became evident to them and an important part of establishing outcomes for their courses that were in concert with the curriculum. In this instance, the community bond and the awareness of this interdependence motivated the faculty to become better teachers. This community of faculty elected to extend the study into the spring semester and asked other department faculty to join. The continuation of the study is testimony to the value of the experience and the strength of the community that was constructed.

When we look more closely at the actions of the faculty, we recognized they created a community focused on inquiry. The faculty inquired about assessment together and attained a better relationship between them as well as their relationship to the students in their classes. As was evident throughout this project, inquiry is not limited to the laboratory. Following Dewey's notion, inquiry is a natural process of living and, as he stated, inquiry is the directed transformation of an indeterminate situation into one that is determinate and converts elements of the original situation into a unified whole (Dewey, 1938). For Dewey, inquiry occurs as people act into the world so as to make a difference and to take into account the effects our actions have. The efforts of the faculty involved with the project indicated a willingness to adopt an attitude of curiosity and openness about the assessment process and how to become better teachers in the process.

Creating a culture of inquiry is consistent with Banta's (2008) perspective, which maintains that assessment shares many of the features of inquiry since it begins with the questions and moves along to data collection and analysis. Assessment is a kind of research which focuses on what institutions and teachers do and what students are capable of demonstrating. It is only natural that the faculty in this study became a community of inquirers as they collected data and reflected on their practice.

Teaching and learning are two terms that have been linked in the literature for several decades and have attracted attention from both researchers and administrators (Becker & Andrews, 2004). As faculty focus their inquiry on how students learn, they are capable of developing and extending their capacity to teach. The Center for Scholarship of Teaching and Learning at Indiana University has found that faculty make improvements in undergraduate learning by exploring a variety of approaches and reflect on questions about student learning derived from their own experiences in the classroom. For the faculty of Indiana University, the scholarship of teaching and learning is self-renewing and self-broadening. The University believes as its faculty members address more learning outcomes and explore more alternative learning environments, they come to use more diverse and increasingly sophisticated techniques to examine the effectiveness of their strategies.[2]

What we find noteworthy is the joint nature of the action of teachers and students. As we indicated above, outcomes assessment in concerned with what students learn and what teachers do. These are not mutually exclusive as there is continuity in the relationship between teachers' actions and students' learning or outcomes. As we found in our faculty discussions, there was less time spent in talking about assessment as a program imposed by the external world and more time spent focusing on becoming effective teachers so that students may become effective learners. Coming to the realization that this is the central focus of assessment was clearly helpful to our group and reminded us that it did, indeed, have a place in our teaching practices.

Our inquiry into teaching and learning and the role of assessment continues. The faculty have not yet found a satisfactory answer to alternatives to rubrics in measuring student performance, especially in the area of measuring creativity. In the spring semester faculty will move away from the template they used in the fall. The idea is that by encouraging each faculty member

to design their own rubric it would allow for more freedom in making decisions about measurement. Then faculty can focus more precisely on the course content and develop more refined measures with their assignments. However, the faculty decided they would share their rubrics and outcomes standards for their assignments and give each other feedback on what they developed before they are shared with students. We feel this is further evidence of the quality of the community that has been formed through this study, and how our community has learned to use dialogue to sustain and strengthen their community and their practice.

Our findings are consistent with Andrade (2005) who found the strengths of rubrics lie in the ability to clarify learning goals, design instruction that addresses the goals, and provide students with feedback. Like our study group, Andrade raised the issue of validity and noted that educators should be concerned with the quality of the rubric. It is logical to assume that there are good rubrics and those that are less effective and incapable of providing a reliable measure of student performance. It is our contention that faculty will need support and encouragement to develop and refine reliable and valid rubrics or grading criteria. This support may come from within our department, the institution, and through the faculties' continued scholarship. It is also reasonable to assume that rubrics are dynamic and must change as teachers encounter new information, new students, and face the challenges of the environment of which they are a part. We learned that rubrics are not assessment. Rubrics are no more than instruments or tools that help us go about the business of establishing standards and measuring performance. Assessment comes about as we think purposefully about what goes on in our classrooms and across the institution to contribute to our students' development as educated citizens.

_____

[2] http://www.indiana.edu/~sotl/community.html.

## CONCLUDING REMARKS

Ted Marchesse who is the former Vice-President of the American Association for Higher Education stated, "assessment is a rich conversation about student learning." This statement rang true in our study as our conversation and dialogues where imbued with ideas, aspirations, and critique about what they do and can do better. Communication between colleagues has the potential to free us from grammatical confusion about such things as outcomes assessment. Consistent with a communication perspective, dialogue worked by allowing us to create a new language about assessment and apply it to our teaching theories and practices.

We found outcomes assessment is not something faculty should fear and more importantly it should not be imposed upon faculty. Faculty are more than capable of constructing a culture of assessment that establishes meaningful outcomes to assist them and their students move towards attainment. The strength of this study was its openness and the level of active participation the faculty engaged in. Assessment can serve as the means to bring faculty together to inquire about their teaching practices and see the interdependence of the objects, ideas, and people that make up their institution. We have found renewed energy and enhanced our relationships with one another by embracing assessment rather than taking a defensive stance. Assessing our teaching, student learning, and the efficacy of our curriculum is what the academy asks of us and we see it as our responsibility to fulfill this request.

## REFERENCES

Andrade, H (2000). Using Rubrics to Promote Critical Thinking and Learning. *Current Issues in Education Vol. 4, No. 4.*

Angelo, T. (2000) Transforming Departments into Productive Learning Communities. In Lucas, A. (Ed.) *Leading Academic Change: Essential Roles for Department Chairs.* New York: Jossey Bass Publishers.

Banta, T. (2008) The Power of Partnerships in Assessment. Unpublished paper presented at Texas A&M Assessment Conference February 19, 2008, College Station Texas.

Bateson, G. (1972) *Steps to an Ecology of the Mind: Collected Essays in Anthropology, Psychiatry, Evolution, and Epistemology.* San Francisco: Chandler Publishing.

Becker, W., & Andrews, M. (Eds.) (2004) *The Scholarship of Teaching and Learning in Higher Education: Contributions of Research Universities.* Bloomington, IN: Indiana University Press.

Chetro-Szivos, J. (2006) The New Challenges for Intercultural Encounters Post 9-11. In Sides, C. (Ed.), *Freedom of Information in a Post 9-11 World.* Amityville, NY: Baywood Publishing Company.

Cronen, V. & Chetrro-Szivos, J. (2001) Pragmatism as a Way of Inquiring with Special Reference to a Theory of Communication and the General Form of Pragmatic Social Theory. In Perry, D. (Ed.) *American Pragmatism and Communication Research.* Mahwah, NJ: Lawrence Erlbaum Associates, Inc. Publishers.

Dewey, J. (1938) *Logic the Theory of Inquiry,* New York: Holt and Company.

Krippendorf, K. (1977) Information Systems Theory and Research: An Overview. In Ruben, B.D. (Ed.), *Communication Yearbook 1 (pp. 149-171).* New Brunswick, NJ: Transaction Books.

Pearce, W. B. (1989) *Communication and the Human Condition.* Carbondale, IL: Southern Illinois University Press.

## Appendix

*Rubric for COMM 1105 Systems & Theories    Assignment    Communication Theory & Popular Culture Presentation*

| | Beginning 1 | Developing 2 | Accomplished 3 | Exemplary 4 | SCORE |
|---|---|---|---|---|---|
| To work in pairs to develop an 8-12 minute presentation on an assigned communication theory or concept | Description of identifiable performance reflecting a beginning level of performance | Description of identifiable performance reflecting development and movement toward mastery of performance | Description of identifiable performance reflecting mastery of performance | Description of identifiable performance reflecting the highest level of performance | |
| To further students' understanding of a concept or theory of communication by requiring them to "teach" it to the class | Description of identifiable performance reflecting a beginning level of performance | Description of identifiable performance reflecting development and movement toward mastery of performance | Description of identifiable performance reflecting mastery of performance | Description of identifiable performance reflecting the highest level of performance | |
| To use some aspect of popular culture (i.e.: movie, sitcom, magazine article, self-help book, etc.) to compliment students' presentation of the assigned concept/theory to the class | Description of identifiable performance reflecting a beginning level of performance | Description of identifiable performance reflecting development and movement toward mastery of performance | Description of identifiable performance reflecting mastery of performance | Description of identifiable performance reflecting the highest level of performance | |
| To enhance students' self-presentation skills | Description of identifiable performance reflecting a beginning level of performance | Description of identifiable performance reflecting development and movement toward mastery of performance | Description of identifiable performance reflecting mastery of performance | Description of identifiable performance reflecting the highest level of performance | |
| To develop a concise, informative handout that summarizes the students' understanding of the communication theory/concept and serves as a study guide for the final exam | Description of identifiable performance reflecting a beginning level of performance | Description of identifiable performance reflecting development and movement toward mastery of performance | Description of identifiable performance reflecting mastery of performance | Description of identifiable performance reflecting the highest level of performance | |

# Check One: *Tutor Hat, Teacher Hat, Facilitator Hat, Some/All/None of the Above*

## Meesh McCarthy & Erin O'Brien

*University of Massachusetts Boston*

meesh.mccarthy@umb.edu • erinm.obrien@umb.edu

**Abstract:** This autoethnographic essay uses a recent conference experience to delve into questions of process-oriented center-tutor identity. Through multiple lenses and descriptors, we attempt to reveal some of the intricate negotiations that characterize our multi-hatted educative work as tutors, teachers, and workshop facilitators within the UMass Boston community. We argue that the current context of increasing acceptance and recognition of writing center tutor authority and expertise necessitates a reexamination of tutor integrity, tutor/informant roles, and the tutor as a complex self. Anecdotal evidence from the conference presentation, workshop negotiations, and actual tutorials flesh out these autoethnographic snapshots. We forego closure by posing a fresh set of problematic questions, stemming from our new insights.

## I. INTRODUCTION: WELCOME TO THE CONTACT ZONE

### 1. Choosing A Hat (Or Not)

When reading journal articles which hat(s) does a reader unconsciously or consciously choose? Which hat(s) does the same reader choose in paper-writing conferences? When readers look at the title of this essay, which hats (e.g., tutor, teacher, student, workshop facilitator, tutee, writing center director, and/or other) do they instinctively wear?

We explicitly point out the complicated nature of a reader's and academic's hats and roles because this paper examines our complex roles and identities as Reading, Writing, and Study Strategies Center tutors at a university (University of Massachu-

Meesh McCarthy's and Erin O'Brien's official roles in Academic Support Programs include Reading, Writing, and Study Strategies Center, and Graduate Writing Center tutors; and First Year Seminar, and Critical Reading and Writing teachers. In Meesh McCarthy's other hats she has been involved in many undertakings of the University's General Education Program. She studied Composition at UMass Boston. Erin O'Brien earned two degrees (History, Applied Linguistics) from UMass Boston. She has taught, tutored, and offered professional development services in: Higher education, special needs, bilingual education, and adult literacy. She never leaves home without her tutor cap. The authors would like to gratefully acknowledge the time and patient support of Susan Irvings and Mark Pawlak during the writing of this paper. They also wish to recognize the contributions of Irene Ezedi, Ingrid Hungerford, Shelly Karren, Ify Malo, and Jacklyn Partyka to the Center for the Improvement of Teaching presentation from which this larger discussion stemmed. Cynthia Jahn and Polly Welsh provided welcome encouragement. Erin deeply appreciates Mitch Zakrzewski's herculean patience on the home front.

setts Boston) and in a larger context which increasingly recognize reading and writing center tutors as having expertise about the writing process and the expertise to assist with the writing process. Particularly, we are calling into question academia's and our own former notions of writing center[1] tutor-identity and -authority.

## 2. Tutor Identity and Autoethnography

Pratt (1998) uses Guaman Poma's multilingual, cross-cultural, and multi-authoritied message to the King—*The First New Chronicle and Good Government* (1613)[2], a message apparently never read by its intended audience—as a prime example of a text created in the *"contact zone."* Pratt defines "contact zone" as "social space... where cultures meet, clash, and grapple with each other, often in contexts of highly asymmetrical relations of power" (p. 173). Poma's is a model *"autoethnographic* text, ... a text in which people undertake to describe themselves in ways that engage with representations others have made of them" (p. 175, emphasis in the original).

We situate ourselves in Pratt's contact zone because this approach facilitates our expression of tutor values through cross-commentary, subversion of definitions, dependence on simultaneous systems of authority, questioning of identity, and recognition of the multiple forms of epistemology and literacy present in the environments in which we and other writing center tutors are situated (see Bawarshi

& Pelkowski, 2008, pp. 88-93, for example). This approach allows us to inform about the writing center tutor role (which we focus on here, rather than on the subject/content tutor) as multi-faceted without abandoning the issue of tutor-integrity.

The literature recognizes the writing center tutor as non-singular. Recently, Murphy and Sherwood (2008) reaffirmed this characterization (and, indirectly, they echo Pratt and Poma) with their initial claim in *The St. Martin's sourcebook for writing tutors*: "Tutoring is contextual. [It]... takes place within a number of sociocultural and interpersonal contexts that lend... complexity to the tutor's role (p. 1, emphasis in the original). We are not authoring the first "point of entry into the dominant circuits of print culture" for the writing center tutor (Pratt points out that autoethnographic texts often take on this duty), yet we do implicate ourselves as being multiply informed, like Poma (trained and educated by both his Inca culture and the conquering Spanish one) (Pratt, p. 175). For us, emerging recognition of the writing center tutor's knowledge and roles is associated with our multiple and multiplying allegiances and functions. We treat the construction of tutor identity using an autoethnographic approach because, in our morphing (and increasingly more accepting) context, the literature's and the academy's perceptions of tutor roles are inadequate.[3]

## 3. The Tutor as Deliberately Composite

In Reed-Danahay's (1997) positioning of the autoethnography as a post-modern venue, she writes that "the coherent, individual self has been... called into question" (p. 2).

The identity of the writing center tutor is composite, one situated within potentially conflicting expectations of the complementary roles that the tutor fills. In other words, the hat-switching tutor deliberately shifts among complementary roles to work

---

[1] We often omit the word 'reading' from our discussion of reading and writing centers to avoid repeated qualifications. 'Reading' is the first word in our Center's full title because the staff do not recognize reading and writing as dichotomous processes, and because working on reading is an appropriate use of tutorials. Much of what we claim can be applied to the reading-writing process.

[2] A scanned facsimile of Poma's *Chronicle* is viewable at *El sitio de Guaman Poma* at http://www.kb.dk/permalink/2006/poma/info/es/frontpage.htm.

effectively with students; recognition of this fluidity and of its necessity is obscured due to constructions of tutors' identities (by dominant and non-dominant groups on campus) which stem from the ways in which each group is situated. And, dominant, in the writing center tutor case, is encased in shifting hierarchies. Students and their advocates rightfully perceive the tutor as serving the tutee. Teachers to some extent must identify tutors as those who will help students perform and progress in the teachers' course(s). The academy (and to some extent the writing center itself) constructs tutor-identity as a composite, and tutors are in part employees.

Each of the above constructions of the tutor relies on the various dominant-groups' repositioning of the other groups in the university. When a tutee physically hands a paper draft to a tutor, knowledge from these multiple roles and about these multiple positionings influence the tutor's effort to return the paper to tutee control. Striving for an impossible single identity approach would be unhealthy for both tutor and tutee. Yet, the tutor needs to take on

---

[3] Both authors are tutors and workshop facilitators for the Reading, Writing, and Study Strategies Center, and for the Graduate Writing Center, both of which are housed in Academic Support Programs at UMass Boston. Both authors have also taught Academic Support Programs' Critical Reading and Writing courses and First Year Seminars. Our roles as professional tutors/teachers has become connected with a tradition in which we provide tutoring and conferencing workshops for other tutors and teachers, drop in writing workshops for students, specific reading and writing in-class workshops for both undergraduate and graduate courses, and writing workshops for graduate student orientations. (Thus, we are Inca, King, or Poma depending on the time of day, and sometimes all three at once.) In the tutoring programs that have shaped our identities, tutor and tutee do not have the same student status (i.e., graduate students tutor undergraduate students, professional tutors tutor graduate students); however, the initial roles of tutors in the Reading, Writing, and Study Strategies Center are complicated by the fact that tutors are students—albeit with a different status, themselves.

a great deal of authority to successfully define and shift among the multiple hats s/he wears.

## 4. Our "Contact Zone" Code: Lack of Linearity and of Systematic Links among Terms

This is not a narrative which provides an all-encompassing and exhaustive ethnography or auto-biography of the writing center tutor. It is a disjointed invitation for readers to wear *their* multiple hats while reading this text. We recognize that our self-referential definitions will be an inadequate whole. Just as theater audiences suspend logic while watching a lone actor play alternating roles in a one-person performance, we suspended much of the conventional logic and expectations of the uni-directional essayist tradition to get at the greater truth of our 'composite selves': Multi-hatted informant—Inca/ruler, King, and Inca/Poma. Likewise, the authors expect that readers are continuing to collect a closet full of various, complementary hats—e.g., tutor, teaching assistant, teacher, writing center director—over time. And so, in the spirit of sharing this snapshot auto-ethnography we invite you to be prepared to switch and choose among your hats, or to wear many at once.

One way to read this paper is to think of it as loosely resembling a DNA double helix. Some things are discussed on their own terms, and some are defined in terms of their mirror image (across the helix). Our paper attempts to echo Poma's manipulation of standard Spanish chronicles to both tell his story and to critique the dominant discourse. Like Poma, we have inverted, reversed, subverted, and appropriated concepts for our purposes. Our logic is that it is more useful to use a broken code switching model than to limit ourselves to linearity. Our code unzips and can be reordered to form new sequences and ideas. We appropriate the ability to separate and regroup as we reconstruct identity. We view this as a performative text, as both product and process. When choosing among hats, readers may want to think of our code's building blocks as epistemology, authority, and negotiation, whereas tutor-identity, tutor-integrity, tutor's investment in his/her role, and the tutor as informant are the meeting/linkage points on the helix.

## 5. *Operational Definitions as Linkages*

What is paramount to the operational definitions of these linkage points which will be incrementally unpacked in this paper? For now, we merely offer broadly defined components of our "Four I's":

• Tutor Integrity:

a) consists of self-respect to follow ethical commitments, even within a context of inappropriate definitions and expectations;
b) depends on commitment to students' long-term benefits;
c) relies on experiential credibility, which simultaneously frames tutor integrity and identity;
d) depends on adherence to non-authoritative authority, an adherence from which tutor identity also stems;
e) manifests in negotiations with teachers and tutees, which connects it to authority.

• Tutor Identity:

a) is associated with the recognition of the tutor as responsible for fostering the knowledge-making process and the development of thinkers, writers, and learners, rather than of products;
b) stems from a tutor's responsibility to his/her pedagogy, which is linked to epistemology;
c) stems from a tutor's commitment to fluid identity as core on which integrity depends;

d) becomes increasingly complex as tutors realize that their identity enables them to witness in tutees what students attempt to hide from teachers, which reframes a tutor's epistemology insofar as this animates informant roles;
e) relies on ethnographic discourses and models, no matter which context/role we are in.

• Tutor Investment:

a) is associated with commitments to do and to be, and, conversely, to not be and not do; (as such, we are invested in the other three 'I's'; for example, in a multi-positioned identity, as is indicated by the willingness to semi-abandon a traditional paper writing process);
b) is aligned with an identity derived from professional integrity, or soundness, which provides our own norms for determining the nature of our professional commitments and fundamental praxis;
c) is fundamental to the tutor in the process of negotiating, because it is part of the dynamic between identity and integrity.

• Tutor/Informant:

a) Our tutor identity and integrity rely on a tutor's informant role/status;
b) The core transferable components of our identities as educators are the tutor's epistemology, which allows the tutor to inform, and the tutor's authority;
c) Tutors who inform (even implicitly) their communities about tutors' identity foster the learning process.

These four qualities are like compatible fabrics which we weave together to form our coherent selves and corresponding authority. Regardless of the particular hat in question, we use the same basic fabrics with different patterns. As we describe later, these linkages manifest themselves during the deliberate hat shifts and sharing that we perform.

## 6. The Literature and General Definitions upon Which We Rely and Which We Defy

Until quite recently, frank discussion of tutors' identity and authority appeared in some newsletters, but less commonly in scholarly work. The sources of this barren landscape are legion and often indisputably self-evident: The sheer variety of tutoring contexts and roles, institutional and professional marginalization, variability in professional credentials and standards easily come to mind. Consequently, the majority of scholarly publications are not authored by tutors; writing and learning center directors and professors pervade. In addition, a mere handful of publications which include a variety of submissions from college-level writing tutors, such as *The Writing Lab Newsletter* and *Praxis*, dominates the field.

The prevailing image of tutors as peripheral 'service' workers (Gordon, 2006) is less powerful than it once was, but it continues to defy defiance—with lamentable consequences—partly because the image and state of the literature mutually reinforce each other. As composite selves, we actively compose our identities in the midst or entanglement of the dominant norming compositions of academic identities and status in a hierarchy. Gordon's lament has non-universal application, just as our definitions are inadequate. Our immediate environment (a very process oriented center) accepts a more accurate definition of tutors' value, which complicates our position. We are valued both as tutors and teachers and we therefore must make deliberate choices to maintain the integrity of our roles. For example, when, as staff of our writing center, we offer a workshop on writing conferences for faculty, are we wearing a tutor or faculty hat? Or facilitator? Sometimes we juggle our hats; at other times we balance them. The authors' experiences disallow them from viewing the hats as either/or options.

## II. THE CENTER AT THE CENTER OF THIS PAPER

Any ethnography needs a context. Ours, the Reading, Writing, and Study Strategies Center, is a story in its own right. We begin to tell our multi-hatted stories by providing an incomplete description of Center-culture.

Simply by joining the staff, we enter a vibrant, creative, and dynamic community. To thrive in it, we invariably embrace an acculturation characterized by enthusiastic mutual support. Just as Freire (1990) encouraged teachers to be learners and students to be teachers, staff members freely ask for, offer, and agree to assist each other. *Non*-fix-shop talk is a major activity. This collaboration and mutual support are made possible because tutors work in a common space that facilitates spontaneous conversation, as well as opportunities for unobtrusive observation. Our co-Directors spend time in "the Center" throughout the day in ways that are universally helpful. In a very real way, the Center itself creates conditions for the overriding culture of mentoring, apprenticeship, and respect; the ongoing professional development and transparency foster a strong sense of identity, integrity, and investment that allow us to assert our sense of appropriate tutor-tutee authority. The Center-culture, as well as our own investment in the educative process, support and facilitate efforts to 'catch' ourselves when we overstep our bounds.

An essential component of the Center's culture of investment, informing, integrity, and identity are the weekly staff meetings. These morph weekly as needed—from meetings which allow staff to share strategies for working with struggling tutees, role-plays, and writing drafts for new Center-authored resources for students, to meetings about requests from teachers asking for workshops for students, and announcements and calls for papers. As this list indicates, the Center's context—a public university that is committed to service and research—compels it and its apprentices to fill multiple roles.

Through the process of reexamining the Center's workshop and presentation planning, we have discovered that the cross-hatted tutor is writing (and acting) a sort of autoethnography squared; s/he exists in a positive feedback loop. To successfully work with students, teachers, tutees, and themselves, tutors in the contact zone need to be double informants and autoethnographers (rather than purporting to relinquish authority). As someone who is able to change hats, the tutor bears the responsibility for both having and not having authority, for informing (and sometimes educating) the taught and the teacher. S/he is sending messages to the Spanish and the Inca, messages about teachers, tutees, tutors, and students. However, tutorials (and tutor/tutee meetings with teachers) are not primarily intended to develop an understanding of a tutor's role, because the construction of the *tutee's* role is and should be the main focus of tutorials. Thus, left venue-less, we as tutors have taken to subverting the workshops that we provide for our larger community.

The problematic characterization of the tutor as effaced repair-shop worker, mythical quick-fixer upper, and authority-less grammar checker is what we debunk in our workshops. Traditionally, Center tutors pass the tutor-facilitator-teacher hats to the unsuspecting attendees and instead take on the role of the student-tutees. This shift allows us facilitators to resist association with single identities, and it implicates the attendees. The reversal is appreciated by the community as it allows us to form a

united front to broaden the recognition of tutors as active participants in the teaching of individual-student-writing. This is particularly relevant as writing centers become teacher resources—a trend confirmed by Harris's (n.d.) directions to readers: "[S]ee what writing lab services are available to assist you in your teaching and your own professional development" (para. 5). We have come to realize that our workshops are often autoethnographic fora, similar to our exploration here.

Workshops allow us to tackle epistemological and pedagogical questions of the authority, power, and identities associated with multiple instructional hats. Tutor identity, knowledge, and authority are too fragmented and morphable to allow single definitions. So, as we deconstruct tutor epistemology and authority based on *our* context, we do so within the confines of an autoethnographic text and dialogue appropriate for the cross-hatting, non-coherent tutor. Higher education needs use a variety of approaches to reach a fuller understanding of the larger relationship among the tutor's roles; we provide an explanation of *Negotiating the Academic Hat Trick: Exploring Strategies For and From Teaching, Tutoring, and Workshop Facilitating*, our 2008 Center for the Improvement of Teaching workshop as an example of how this might occur.

## 1. Center Tutors' Roles at Conferences

Conferences serve as more formal opportunities to present Center tutors' roles to the community. Our *Hat* presentation is part of an annual tradition in which Center staff join forces to respond to calls for presentations. (The authors have been part of six Center for the Improvement of Teaching conference presentations.[4]) Center tutors anticipate the yearly conference. This year

---

[4] For example, *How Long Is An Hour?: Dispelling the Myth of the Quick Fix Tutorial* and *Negotiating the Void: Moving Between Informal and Formal Writing*.

we opted to concentrate on unpacking three roles that Center staff serves in the UMass Boston community: Tutors, workshop facilitators, and teachers. When community members ask what Center tutors do, we often sense that they expect us to declare a single role. So, we welcome the opportunity to inform and perhaps demystify what we do. Outside the contact zone of Academic Support Programs we repeatedly encounter that oversimplified "coherent, individual self" that we beg to "call... into question" (Reed-Danahay, p. 2). These tacit models tend to split our multi-faceted roles into either-or dichotomies that can obscure some hats and amplify others.

The conference proposal serves as an autoethnographic snapshot. Our panel chose its words carefully. The final title plays on the theme of wearing many hats combined with the sports notion of a "hat trick"—an occasion when a hockey or soccer player scores three goals in a single game. With the abstract, which "invite[d] participants to explore the challenges and opportunities of serving in multiple instructional roles" (O'Brien et al., 2008, p. 1) the panel strove to say what it actually meant to do so that it could deliver on its stated intentions.

Our planning process informs about the ways in which we contest the dominant characterization, functions, and behaviors that the academy ascribes to our tutor role. Our multi-faceted roles and construction of authority became evident to us as we reexamined our collaboration. Each person decides if and how s/he will participate. A few volunteers draft a working proposal and send it out for feedback. After the round of feedback, volunteers polish the proposal and submit it.

## 2. Our Negotiated Process during Presentation Planning and Actual 'Presentation'

Habermas's (1987) framework of communicative action helps describe the normative qualities of Center collaboration. We speak, listen, evaluate, and decide from the presupposition that all of these actions are "oriented to reaching understanding" (p. 27). Consequently, we reject and accept our own and others' "validity claims" on the basis of reasoned counterclaims and evidence (p. 27). Insofar as the panel members honored their intention to converse freely, they "proceed[ed] in the expectation that they can achieve a rationally motivated agreement and can coordinate their plans and actions" (p. 27). According to Habermas, this "linguistic medium of reaching understanding gains the power to bind the wills of the responsible actors" (p. 27). The tutors *reason* out a single plan by freely *binding wills* to what they honestly see as the most valid rationale for a given project. The open, non-coercive reasoning process of claims and evidence is an essential stage in a process that our panel continually enacted and refined.

Our integrity is further manifested by the continuity between the Center's "ways with words" (Heath, 1983) and the presentation process. We, the authors of this paper, had the authority to preserve the expert-audience participant structure, but we also had and exercised our legitimate option to impose an alternative presentation characterized by dialogue among equals. In this way, by risking inviting people to move out of the familiar conference comfort zone into new interactional relations, we obviated the need to consider 'keeping' audience attention and other pitfalls of normative educative discourse models, for example, the Initiation-Response-Evaluation (Hicks, 1996) paradigm.

Four days before the conference we were still relying on e-mails to unify the multiple purposes that the panel associated with the presentation. Excerpts from the e-mail exchange convey a pattern of reasoning that approximates Habermas's model of communicative action: Our co-panelists:

"We discussed a tentative 'outline'…. Disclaimer, we weren't exactly sure what role you… wanted or what you had in mind, so feel free to let us know" (S. Karren, personal communication, January 22, 2008). Our (the authors') response to the outline reads in part:

> If we do the …role plays consecutively people might be more reluctant to participate…there will be observers…. We might… not set folks up for a meaningful…conversation…. [I]f we've switched to the three…skits it seems …we've taken on a lot more work. Erin and I did a role play at the FYS/IS debriefing and …even though we did not script [it]… we spent much time meeting…. But [it's possible that we are]…. not fully following [your reasoning]. (M. McCarthy, person communication, January 23, 2008)

And it was this dimension that was a strength and vulnerability. It was the sense in which the panelists most worked as tutors, even when no tutees were present. While everyone had a voice, all panelists deferred to one another to the extent that the selection of one out of a short list of possible approaches occurred shortly before the presentation was scheduled. Early on the morning of the presentation, the authors were scurrying to gather the physical equipment—flip charts, scrap-paper-hats, and copies of debriefing questions—necessitated by the final choice. Thus equipped, the authors met with their co-panelists and filled them in on the last nuts-and-bolts steps.

This decidedly normative vision "approximates" free open speech because there is at least the speakers' "intention of openness, even if the present level of [discursive] development of individuals or society does not actually permit it" (Young,

1992, p. 51). This negotiation style reflected how we collaborate in the Center: We did not assert our concerns and alternatives because we were more experienced but because of our experience we were able to present an argument for a different presentation plan more in keeping with the panelists' initial shared priorities. In this respect, our communicative styles and values powerfully approximate Habermas's model of communicative action. Our multiple hats and experiences provide a broad epistemology, pedagogy, and recognition of others' composite sets of knowledge and experience.

## 3. The Center at the Presentation

While we were officially tagged as a panel, the presenters did not sit together at the front of the room. Believing in the importance of a purposeful interactive presentation that delivered what had been advertised was paramount, the panelists revised the typical format. Late arrivals would have found it impossible to distinguish the presenters from the participants. Three groups were formed, consisting of both panelists and presenters for the three instructional contexts: Workshop, tutorial, and instructor-student writing conference. An interactive design necessarily demands that facilitators integrate *all* participants into the pre-determined plan. Within each group, the panelists-participants took on the unscripted tutee/student roles, intending to recreate some of the more challenging interactions the panelists have encountered. Attendee-participants acted as workshop facilitators, tutors, and an instructor in a writing conference.

Despite our workshop subverting, we recognize the academy's participant structures and norming discourse can "constrict the flow of dialogue and perpetuate ideological and epistemological distortions" (O'Brien, 2000, p. 3), creating a forced false consensus. Yet we (and many other tutors)

do not uncritically accept the asymmetrical relations and discourse that are imposed. The increased demand for workshops for and from various members of our community suggests that we are not the only ones questioning the dominant paradigm.

Why is it hard to bring these questions of tutor identity to the surface in the context of academia? Young's discussion of constrained speech resonates with our self understanding of the pervasive difficulty with explicitly, openly addressing these intertwined questions of identity, integrity, investment, and informant status. In the academy's microcosm—the classroom—and throughout its larger contexts we find "dialogue constrained by limitations, by teachers' authority, by taboos and no-go zones" (Young, p. 47), where "authority replaces reason" (p. 48). In our case, the product of dominant, normative discourse is a distorted representation of fragmented identities that obscure or camouflage our 'natural' multi-hatted coherent self from public images, symbols, and associations. Thus some of our professional integrity derives from the value of consistency, and we continually strive to act with this intention of transparency and openness with every hat we wear. This dimension of our practice, we suspect, can promote less distorted fora and framing of epistemologies.

## III. THE CENTER TUTOR IN CONTEXT

Here, we invite the reader to renavigate the cross-hatted tutor's 'Four I's', while focusing on tutor epistemology and authority. This section degrades/upgrades into a series of vignettes. We expect the hat-switching reader to actively read (Quinn and Irvings, 1997) as we move through the spectrum from formal writing to 'showing not telling' in the narrative form often used by tutors when they are addressing their peers and other community members in

newsletters.

## 1. The Center Tutor's Fluid Identity

Our workshops and other experiences lead us to self-define as chameleons and switch hatters, with fluid roles, multiplicity, multiple connections among roles, and a complex coherence. Tutors' epistemologies are informed/shaped by the academic context and thus, informed by instruction as well as tutoring experience. The exclusion of all the abilities, authority, and experience associated with teachers from the tutor's pedagogy is therefore problematic. Tutors cannot facilitate learning if the tutor's total separation from teacher is categorically given more importance than the tutee's progress. To maintain integrity we daily renavigate the blurred social construction of the 'tutor'; we resist the construct of tutor as proofreader/fixer, yet we also resist the construction of tutor as non-teacher (in the informal sense).

## 2. Cross-hatting Fluid Identity and Epistemologies

What is happening as tutors' effacement (in the norming descriptions) diminishes? When his/her role and contribution are no longer associated with invisibility, a lack of authority and autonomy, and subordination, what is the writing center tutor expected to know?

The expectations are both appropriate and enormous. For example, Garbus (2005) argues that writing tutors of graduate students need more interdisciplinary expertise, and the ability to make students experts in and informants about their own field. Kimball (2007), both an undergraduate student and a peer tutor, defines tutors as those who "wear many hats as diagnosticians, audience members, devil's advocates, and guides," and as those who acquire a great deal of knowledge about becoming "better students" from wearing the tutor hat (para. 2, 1). Harris (n.d.) claims that tutors can be "cultural informants" for non-Native speakers of English (para. 3; we would argue that no native speakers of Academic English exist and that all tutees need informants). In our context, tutors work in tandem with students, other tutors, course instructors, directors, and teaching assistants, and are often coaches, role models, and/or workshop facilitators, formally, while wearing her/his tutor hat. Although they help individual students with courses researched and designed by others, effective writing center tutors are *informal* teachers of writing and the individual student-writer's process. Additionally, the writing center tutor can have other, *formal* roles—teacher, assistant, workshop facilitator, student—at the same academy. The literature indicates that expectations about tutors' knowledge have expanded, but the tutor with this more appropriate epistemology must still rely on the student as informant to be more fully effective.

One possible outcome of the poorly defined multi-faceted tutor identity/role is the chance that a tutor may intentionally or inadvertently try her/his hand at "play[ing] ... professor" (Jacoby, 2008, p. 148). Another possibility is the replacement of the tutor-tutee constructed session by a situation like that which Neff (1999) recounts: The "session is controlled by what the teacher said... and... marked on [the] paper. The teacher may be physically absent..., but her authority is overwhelmingly present. [The tutor]... decodes the instructor's marginal comments and interprets them... using mini-grammar lessons" (para. 6). The Center context helps us to avoid these pitfalls by being honest to our ethical and pedagogical values and clarifying these to our tutees. At each meeting we negotiate the session's agenda by sharing authority. This stance is derived from our core conviction that shared negotiating power is ethically and pragmatically valid. By sharing in decision-making, by asking

and listening, we necessarily minimize the chance that we act as a second or substitute instructor. Strengthening and maintaining our integrity requires investment in ongoing critical self-reflection.

Conversely, when tutees initially and categorically defer to us, we offer ethical and pedagogical reasons for requiring their proactivity, including assuming appropriate responsibility. Often their deference manifests itself indirectly as passivity (e.g., waiting for us to initiate the session), or directly by overtly attributing expert status to us (e.g., "Well, you're the tutor, just tell me what to do"). Regardless of the specific form this passivity takes, we avoid the "despotism of the expert" (Appelbaum, Lidz, & Meisel, as cited in Jacoby, 2008, p. 149) because of our belief that students have at least some of the tools they need to master academic challenges and virtually all of the potential to achieve this mastery. We acknowledge that while we may have knowledge that they need, they have knowledge that we need in order to support them.

## 3. Center Tutor Identity Influences on Teacher Identity and Integrity

The Center's epistemology is informed because tutors all are or were students at UMass Boston—unlike many of the faculty. Our epistemology is informed by politics and expresses itself in deliberately political acts, such as opposition to the deficit mentality (Valencia, 1997, p. xi) and to the banking education which dictates that writing center tutors-tutees work primarily in one direction with tutor as expert, imparting knowledge.

At the Center, most staff members' careers start as graduate students tutoring undergraduates. The possibility of teaching (in multiple programs and disciplines) eventually and frequently opens up, but at this point the crucial investment in the tutor epistemology has already been initiated. In other words, the faculty outlooks/epistemologies of former and current Center tutors are cultivated from the pre-existing matrix of experience, knowing, and constructing knowledge in a sort of Grand Central. We have had the privileged opportunity *and* challenge to keep a hat while acquiring others. Coulbrooke (1999), who self identifies as "a teacher who is also a tutor," argues that this composite renders her capable of empathy, unlike those "GIs [graduate instructors] who… accepted the role of teacher as authority. They didn't have the advantage of being a peer to their students first" (p. 12). Our own experiential credibility as student writers contributes to the efficacy of our work (Nelson, 1991, p. viii). This, combined with the power of disciplined, empathic listening, feed our epistemological resources (Nelson, p. viii). We learn from tutees as a necessary condition whereas faculty learn from students indirectly and incidentally.

Faculty epistemologies tend to be tied to their disciplines and specializations. Tutors' knowledge bases are associated with global academic abilities (e.g., reading and writing) and strategies, including those necessary for navigating the tower's (Shaughnessy, 1976) labyrinthine expectations and taboos. Furthermore, faculty epistemologies are more closely tied with outcomes in the form of expectations for products whereas tutor epistemologies include processes that help construct those products. Nevertheless, tutors need discipline-specific knowledge; they learn how to make use of content especially by accumulating and being informed/informing about knowledge of normative written discourses.

These institutionally determined differences in epistemology can be best seen in the nature of faculty requests for tutor support, including in-class workshops. For example, a sociology teacher asks for a two session tutor-workshop which applies reading and then writing abilities to mass media content analysis. Another teacher requests a workshop to help students unpack the writing-revision process in the context of a graduate nursing course. Faculty rarely if ever ask tutors to supplement content specific information; this is their domain. The Center's domain is global strategies and bridging them into the disciplines for students.

## 4. Tutor Epistemology as Socially Constructed by the Tutee/Informant

A Center apprentice acts on the conviction that students, as "knowing subjects[,]…are expert sources of information for a tutor and themselves… who can productively and proactively work with tutors toward becoming more confident and competent academic writers" (O'Brien, 1993, p. 1). This kind of pedagogical conviction springs from repeatedly engaging with students about their reading and writing processes; in other words, we may wear a 'King' hat when tutees play Poma's informant role.

In the academy, writing fluency is a necessary and highly prized expectation with which many students struggle (Huang, 2004). Some of these struggles derive from distorted, misinformed beliefs about writers and writing. Myths, such as 'good writers only write one draft,' 'revising is a fancy word for editing,' and 'good writers are born' with a magical 'gift,' pose formidable obstacles to basic expectations: Meeting essay due dates and minimum length requirements.

A few years ago one author worked with a tutee who, despite being a conscientious thoughtful person who cared about her education and writing, consistently failed to meet both these expectations. Over a semester of weekly hour-long sessions, this student writer not only progressed in her writing agenda but did so partly by assuming more authority over her writing and tutorials. Her acquisition of technical information about composing was necessary but not sufficient for demonstrating writing proficiency. She increasingly accepted responsibility for taking the sessions and making them her own. Towards the end of the semester she commented that it was "Okay" that sometimes her tutor's analogies and explanations were unclear and incomplete: "There are no problems with what you talked about. I was looking at the paper, thinking about what you said about elaborating and stuff. I can't take you home with me, so I imagined what you'd say" (O'Brien, 1993, p. 18). One of the strategies she came to expertly employ was wearing a reader hat when she was revising: "I asked myself questions. I put myself as the reader and felt I could say more" (p. 19); this was after being introduced to the notion of reader- and writer-based texts (Flower, 1979).

By the end of that semester, she initiated sessions with a predetermined task for her tutor, such as "Can you read this and find my thesis!?" Instead of hesitating and doubting the existence of her thesis, as she did earlier in the semester, she knew she had a thesis and appropriately exerted her authority within the relationship. She *informed* that: "I thought about what you said last week about graduating to another… level. I thought maybe that's not so bad…. I benefit from talking about my writing because then I'm aware of the stages I go through" (p. 27). Further, at this point, tutor and tutee both knew they had been successful because the tutee was putting her tutor out of a job. She became more proficient in meeting deadline and length requirements. From such anecdotal evidence, we get a sense of how a tutor's epistemology is powerfully shaped by tutee's self knowledge so that tutors can eliminate some of the guesswork around the former's processes.

Many conventions of tutor roles and identities are framed in contra-distinction to teachers, as if these roles were always fulfilled by different people. That is, each person has his/her own designated role—and only one. Thus, the discourses of multiple hats, of Center-like writing centers, become problematic. An educator's designated *and* de facto hats pose discursive and practical difficulties to the extent that they are counter-normative. For example, Inglis (1997), a tutor who deconstructs her own visit to the writing center as a tutee, claims that "[t]he roles of teacher, tutor, and student are very distinct, yet they become an integral part of each other in the learning and writing process" (p. 11). When describing the tutor-tutee relationship Inglis defines herself as having important knowledge (because her tutor "was completely inexperienced with [Inglis's] specific needs" (p. 11)), and her tutor as a knowledgeable person who "could give me pointers similar to those of a teacher" (p. 12). However, reciprocity is not influential in Inglis's analysis of the context of the "*teacher*-tutor-student *triangle*" (p. 11, emphasis added). Even as someone with two hats herself, Inglis described a *uni*-directional flow of information from teacher to tutor, and from tutor to tutee (p. 11). Ultimately, artificial limits restrict the outcome of the tutorial and the reflection on it.

The diminishing yet pervasive myth of tutoring is that the tutor's epistemology and purpose do not allow him/her to help with a knowledge-making process, and thus, that the tutor has no authority, which distinguishes a tutor from faculty. This simplification is also a factor or condition for tutorial success. An implication of this condition is that a tutor is 'free' from evaluative concerns and issues of power, and thus optimally geared to help students help themselves. In other words, since tutors have no putatively vested interest in the tutees' work/performance, they are free to be neutral. However, what may appear to be 're-linquishing,' or simply no choice to retain/relinquish authority, or a vacuum, is more aptly perceived as embracing different forms of authority and credibility.

## 5. Center-Tutor Defines 'Tutor' Hat by Defining Tutee's Hat

Just as a faculty members' authority is not absolute in a course context, so too tutors' seemingly absolute lack of authority is misleading. The respective natures of the authority of each role are decidedly different; insofar as the instructor's power is centered in/on curriculum and evaluation, there is a gate keeping function.

Scaffolding and meeting students 'where they are' do not fall under some aspects of course-based authority. Furthermore, both tutors and faculty have their own views of authority stemming from their personal pedagogies and professional ethics. Center tutors also have context specific authority regarding the use of tutorials. We have the authority to clarify and insist that tutees behave appropriately. We follow established policies of what we do and do not practice and permit based on clear pedagogical principles and values, which we communicate when tutees are initially unaware of, or resistant to, our expectations (for instance, when tutees' expectations are unrealistic, or pedagogically or socially inappropriate). One of the more critical areas of tutor authority at the Center stems from the 'no quick fix' policy. (For various reasons, a new tutee may expect the tutor to edit drafts—while s/he passively sits and waits.) Center tutors self identify as having the capability to foster the long-term knowledge-making process. Thus, they are comfortable with their expectation that tutees will keep their weekly meeting commitments (and with helping the tutees to subscribe to the same expectation).

We claim the right and responsibility to not settle for student passivity (Nelson, p. viii). Instead, tutorials position tutees as informants about courses, tasks, personal reading and writing processes, and tutee-

expectations; the tutors are likewise informants, about how the long-term process and the student-driven Center-culture put them in a position to learn how to write, read, and think effectively and efficiently. Tutors follow self-imposed limits as they parcel out descriptions of meta-processes that relate to the specific-task work that tutees hope to accomplish over time.

## 6. Tutees vs. Students as Informants of Tutor/Student/Teacher/Confidante

Participants in our *Hat* workshop confirmed that tutors are exposed to "moving targets"—in other words, to student demands, behaviors, and needs that change during tutorials, as more about the students' challenges is unearthed.

As confidante, the tutor is privy to a truer range of tutee behaviors than teachers are allowed to view when those same tutees are wearing their student hats (exclusively) with their teachers. Tutees expose their boredom, lack of preparedness, confusion, excitement about course materials, and their frustration with themselves, classmates, and teachers. As tutorials focus on individuals, the tutor can encourage this self exposure, when it is useful.

A cross-hatting tutor can mentor students with deliberate/fluid shifts, where the tutee ends up wearing the hat of authority. (Center tutors can model a number of reading strategies (e.g., scanning, previewing, and reading the conclusion first) and then ask "If I was sitting next to you on the UMass shuttle bus, and I told you that I had that much material to read by Wednesday, which strategies would you tell me to try?) Or, s/he can swap hats to validate the difficulty of the task being tackled, again making the tutee the authority hat wearer, even as the Center tutor carefully alludes to other hats s/he wears with other students, or to struggling with writing her/himself: "You know, I give my students similar instructions [for a written paper assignment] and they need about a week to understand what is being asked of them. I don't expect them to get it right away, and I'm sometimes glad *I* don't have to write that paper" or, "If you were working with the students in your class, even though you didn't need to write the paper yourself, how would you help them? What would they need to figure out so that they could write the paper?"

Admissions and questions such as these, often impossible in classroom context, position the tutee as informant-with-authority, *even* after self-exposure (e.g., "I haven't kept up with the reading all semester") has occurred.

## 7. Tutor Discards Association with Teacher/Authority Hat

Furthermore, wearing a tutor hat can open more doors into other types of relevant student knowledge that an instructor hat typically will not grant. The profoundly dialogic nature of one-to-one sessions is grounded in the practice of both participants assuming learner (listener) and teacher (talker) roles (Freire, 1990, p. 67).

Tacit assumptions and other ideological notions of what college is about play a powerful role in every aspect of students' academic performance. For example, studies focusing on beliefs and underlying assumptions of what good writers 'do' underscore the profound impact beliefs have on choices (Nelson, p. viii). Conventional course design and participant structures are not intended to accommodate this kind of disclosure/access (Phillips, 1972). In this respect, instructors are left relying mostly on artifacts like tests and essays. Tutors' epistemological possibilities are not constrained in the same way.

In ongoing relationships, tutees directly inform a tutor's epistemology by divulging crucial information about their beliefs, theories, and values pertaining to reading, writing, and other academic capabilities. Thus, by addressing the writer and the text (Zamel, 1985), tutors and tutees have powerful information that can help overcome obstacles such as writer's block and ineffective reading strategies.

## 8. Tutee/Informant Plus Tutor/Informant Equals Writing Center Director/Informed

Tutors inform unofficially because formal channels do not always exist. Tutor authority is not always recognized as exercised. Macauley (2004) reports that tutors at the writing center that he directs subverted a putatively mundane discussion of supplies to respond to his pedagogical guidelines which mandated that tutors read tutees' papers aloud as a way to engage tutees. In this instance, the tutors assert authority through opportunistic resistance, as did Poma.

In Macauley's case, as writing center director, he was able to recognize the tutors' authority and knowledge, and he "began to realize that the training I provided to tutors clearly privileged the verbal, to the exclusion of auditory, tactile, and other learning styles/intelligences" (p. 3). His success relied on the change in hats from director to learner, back to director as he made programmatic changes, and then to informant of the larger tutoring community in *The Writing Lab Newsletter*.

When a tutor observes, listens, and poses appropriate questions, the causes of tutees' strengths and challenges can be named, understood, and addressed effectively. Center-pedagogy recognizes that "we as tutors are neither mind readers nor magicians" (O'Brien, 1993 p. 2).

## 9. Teacher and Students Wear Informant Hat with Tutor/Workshop Facilitator

When a faculty member requests an in-class workshop, an especially multi-hatted informant negotiation is initiated. Workshop facilitators possess the authority to set, offer, and propose the level of three-way negotiation. We ask the faculty to clarify and prioritize their expectations for the workshop. We assess these expectations and propose a blueprint that addresses resources, processes, and outcomes. We exercise another aspect of authority when we propose obtaining students' perceptions of the workshop topics and goals. The conventional practice is for faculty to serve as informant to the facilitator. We reverse and even subvert this typically unquestioned solo role by directly soliciting students' input. Often instructors welcome this additional information even though they are surprised when we suggest collecting it. Faculty report that they come to see their students, their teaching, and writing quite differently and profitably.

Our roles as workshop facilitators are the most pliable of our three hats insofar as the participants, context, and purposes are open to variation. Over the past few years the authors have been invited to facilitate a number of end-of-semester General Education Seminar debriefings. When a group of General Education First Year Seminar faculty requested a practical workshop dealing with one-to-one writing conferencing, one of the authors, E. O'Brien, was asked to facilitate. Here, she briefly reflects on the experience as a cross-hatting predicament:

> I was somewhat apprehensive. I wondered which of my hats had gotten me into this situation: Tutor? First Year Seminar Instructor? Debriefer? All? Which hat(s) did the participants expect me to officially wear? These identity-based questions were from more than just from nerves; practical design considerations were embedded in them, too. But first, I needed to negotiate primarily with myself to settle on the order in which I pre-

sented these hats since I would simultaneously have all of them. Then, I solicited input from the faculty, the First Year Seminar Coordinator, and my Directors.

Like other workshops and debriefings, we saw this request as an opportunity to show writing as a complex process, advance a model of conferencing as student centered, and highlight the participants' own experiential credibility. Consequently, I opted to simultaneously wear all of my hats during the two sessions. Although apprehensive, I still asserted my facilitator authority to invoke a dialogue rather than a discussion, including asking participants to be informants for me. If I took a more predictable path of expert monologue, my identities, investment, integrity, expertise, and the quality of the workshops would have been compromised.

## IV. THE GREENHOUSE: A CONCLUSION WITHOUT CLOSURE

### 1. 'So What?'

Many readers will recognize 'So what?' as a question that tutors use to help their tutees fully articulate implications in conclusions. We now perceive that, although the identity distortion of tutors is easily undone, the tutor needs a specific expertise/authority to negotiate their composite identity carefully.

In our practice, despite outsider perceptions of tutors as semi-subordinate, tutors wield a great deal of authority to maintain the integrity of tutees' learning processes. Our autoethnography allows us to perceive experiential credibility as stemming from an intricate weaving of the 'Four

I's.' The result is a partial subversion of our initial perception of ourselves as tutors.

With our accumulated knowledge and epistemology we use the full range of tutor hats, particularly as we recalibrate agenda-setting authority when long-term tutees have developed their own authority and knowledge about productive tutorials. Center tutees, apprenticed to hat-switching, multiple authorities, and becoming informants, gradually master this limit-setting and dedication to long-term process.

Center tutors have a profound investment in their role. We could not previously explain why, in a brief scenario (a tutor-tutee role play) for Seminar faculty on the complexities of academic composing and negotiated interactions, we so fully engaged in our purported tutor-tutee roles that one of us ended up teaching the other something unexpected and fundamental. We knew from this recent (2007) experience that we can be real tutors and/or tutees anywhere, anytime, but we did not realize what we do now about the intertwined nature of tutor identity and tutor investment.

## 2. Roles in Context

We appropriated Murphy's and Sherwood's claim that *"Tutoring is contextual"* (p. 1), and found that 'tutor' and 'tutee' are also contextual and socially constructed.

To what extent is the tutee's witnessing of a tutor navigating a seemingly ambiguous role beneficial? Does this encourage the student to navigate his/her socially constructed, multiple selves? We suspected that a tutor's success (and, in part, identity) is defined by tutee success. However, we did not understand how the successful tutor unifies fragments of roles as s/he participates in tutorials, nor how this modeling allows the tutee to witness a non-authoritative model of a composite, partly academic self. When tutees realize this, they can use the model as a portal, to navigate their own multi-faceted composite tutee/informant/

student/worker/family-member/learner/community-member selves (*particularly* at our non-traditional university).

A tutor's authority is contextual and morphs when responding to the moving targets tutees provide as they expose their real concerns and challenges. However, the Center tutor can rarely, if ever, presume to claim 'I'm just the messenger,' insofar as her/his polyglot authority, ability to change hats, and the inherently negotiable nature of tutorials preclude such abandonment.

## 3. The Insider and Outsider Views of the Center

The view of the Center as Grand Central from the outside has led to a greater recognition of it as a resource for students and faculty. Yet, we have learned that tutor identity and integrity appear differently through the inside lens.

This examination of our insider status has eased our concern about the ways in which we carefully compartmentalize some of our formal roles (for example, as faculty we do not tutor students in our classes, and we afford our students the same privacy with their tutors as any other tutees); yet, we informally switch hats and behaviors in the tutor, teacher, and (especially) facilitator roles. We have come to realize that we recommend that our students become tutees because we view the Center-contact-zone as a greenhouse where natural, productive hybrids-of-roles can be encouraged. And, we hope that our students become ready to formally assume other roles.

We would like to say to fellow tutors: Remember that there's always someone else with as much potential as you in the room and that you might be teaching alongside your former tutee someday. (We have witnessed this.)

## 4. Further Inquiries

How does the presence of Center-like centers affect student and faculty culture on other campuses? One author often wonders this when she creates Center workshop flyers, and later receives copies of them via a distribution list (in her role as First Year Seminar faculty). What of the apprentices like us, who would not leave the Center? How is a faculty member who retains his/her *formal* tutor hat continually informed and changed by that role? What is the impact of this on our *own* teaching, tutoring, and in-service activities?

There are multiple ways in which we serve as informants to faculty, and some are more direct than others. Through in-class workshops, we tend to indirectly inform instructors not only about their strategies but also about their teaching and curriculum. Faculty responses to our work indicate/confirm they gain greater insight about academic writing, teaching, and their own curriculum from our negotiations and the workshop itself. For example, they have indicated that they would change a writing prompt, or the order of readings, after a workshop. How, in general, has faculty-identity been shaped by increasingly 'present' Center-like centers?

## 5. To Be Continued

We believe that tutors and centers are dynamic and need continual re-reconceptualization. This belief and the previous account are defiantly optimistic in the face of the larger, less stable context of education. But we are products of our Center-context—rough drafts, continually revising ourselves in the midst of our culture, one that we refuse to sabotage.

REFERENCES

Bawarshi, A., & Pelkowski S. (2008). Postcolonialism and the idea of a writing center. In C. Murphy, & S. Sherwood (Eds.), *The St. Martin's sourcebook for writing tutors* (3rd ed). (pp. 79-95). Boston: Bedford/St. Martin's.

Coulbrooke, S. (1999). When the teacher is also the tutor. *The Writing Lab Newsletter,* 24(2), 10-12. Retrieved from http://writinglabnewsletter.org/archives/v24/24.2.pdf

Flower, L. (1979). Writer-based prose: a cognitive basis for problems in writing. *College English,* 41(1), 19-37.

Freire, P. (1990). *Pedagogy of the oppressed.* (M. Ramos, Trans.). New York: Continuum.

Garbus, J. (2005). Tutoring graduate students in the writing center. *Academic Exchange Quarterly,* 9(3), 172-176. Retrieved from Gale Educator's Reference Complete database (A138703683).

Gordon, E. (2006). The state of tutoring in America: changing the culture about tutoring. *Synergy,* 1(2), 1-10. Retrieved from http://www.jsu.edu/depart/edprof/atp/Synergy_1/Syn_5.pdf

Habermas, J. (1987). *The theory of communicative action* (Vol. 2). Lifeworld and System: A Critique of Functionalist Reason. (T. McCarthy, Trans.). Boston: Beacon Press.

Harris, M. (n.d.). *Writing labs: on campus and online.* Retrieved March 25, 2008, from http://www.mhhe.com/socscience/english/tc/pt/harris.htm

Heath, S. (1983). *Ways with words: language, life, and work in communities and classrooms.* Cambridge: Cambridge University Press.

Hicks, D. (1996). Introduction. In D. Hicks (Ed.), *Discourse, Learning and Schooling.* (pp. 1-25). New York: Cambridge University Press.

Huang, J. (2004). Socialising ESL students into the discourse of school science through academic writing. *Language and Education,* 18(2), 97-123.

Inglis, J. A. (1997). The triangle of success in tutoring. *The Writing Lab Newsletter,* 21(6), 10-13. Retrieved from http://writinglabnewsletter.org/archives/v21/21-6.pdf

Jacoby, J. (2008). "The Use of Force": medical ethics and center practice. In C. Murphy, & S. Sherwood (Eds.), *The St. Martin's sourcebook for writing tutors* (3rd ed.). (pp. 141-155). Boston: Bedford/St. Martin's.

Kimball, J. (2007). I'm a student, I'm a tutor, I'm confused!: peer tutor and classroom student. *Praxis: A Writing Center Journal,* 4(2). Retrieved from http://projects.uwc.utexas.edu/praxis/?q=node/149

Macauley, W., Jr., et al. (2004). Paying attention to learning styles in writing center epistemology, tutor training, and writing tutorials. *The Writing Lab Newsletter, 28*(9), 1-5. Retrieved from http://writinglabnewsletter.org/archives/v28/28.9.pdf

Murphy, C., & Sherwood S. (2008). The tutoring process: exploring paradigms and practices. In C. Murphy, & S. Sherwood (Eds.), *The St. Martin's sourcebook for writing tutors* (3rd ed.). (pp. 1-25). Boston: Bedford/St. Martin's.

Neff, J. M. (1999). Something undermining our efforts: what is and isn't working the writing lab. *Journal of College Reading and Learning, 29* (2), 209-. Retrieved from Gale Educator's Reference Complete database (A54805828).

Nelson, M. (1991). *At the point of need: teaching Basic and ESL writers.* Portsmouth, NH: Boynton/Cook.

O'Brien, E., Ezedi, I., Hungerford, I., Karren, S., Malo, I., McCarthy, M., & Partyka, J. (2008, January). Presentation handout presented at the annual Center for the Improvement in Teaching conference, Boston, MA.

O'Brien, E. (2000). *Freire, Habermas, and classroom conversation: a preliminary Discussion.* Unpublished manuscript. Harvard University Graduate School of Education.

O' Brien, E. (1993). *Getting below the tip of the iceberg: student writer case study.* Unpublished manuscript. The University of Massachusetts, Boston, MA.

Phillips, S. (1972). Participant structures and communicative competence: Warm Springs children in community and classroom. In C. Cazden, V. John, & D. Hymes (Eds.), *Functions of language in the classroom.* (pp. 370-394). New York: Teachers College Press.

Pratt, M. (1998). Arts of the contact zone. In V. Zamel, & R. Spack (Eds.), *Negotiating academic literacies: teaching and learning across languages and cultures.* (pp. 171-185). Mahwah, NJ: Lawrence Erlbaum Associates.

Quinn, S., & Irvings, S. (1997). *Active reading in the arts and sciences* (3rd ed.). Boston: Allyn and Bacon.

Reed-Danahay, D. Introduction. (1997). In D. Reed-Danahay (Ed.), *Auto/Ethnography: rewriting the self and the social.* (pp. 1-17). Explorations in anthropology. New York: Berg.

Shaughnessy, M. (1976). Diving in: an introduc-

tion to basic writing. *College Composition and Communication, 27*(3), 234-39.

Valencia, R. (1997). Introduction. In R. Valencia (Ed.) *The evolution of deficit thinking: educational thought and practice.* (pp. ix-xvii). London: Falmer Press.

Young, R. E. (1992). *Critical theory and classroom talk.* D. Corson (Ed.), The Language and Education Library (Vol. 2). Philadelphia: Multilingual Matters.

Zamel, V. (1985). Responding to student writing. *TESOL Quarterly, 19*(1), 79-101.

# First-Generation College Students: Then and Now

## Corinne R. Merritt

*Emmanuel College*

merrittc@emmanuel.edu

**Abstract:** This article seeks to examine past and present first-generation college students, how they have changed demographically, and what colleges can do to assist them in meeting the challenges of higher education. A brief, descriptive memoir of the author as a first-generation college student precedes a concise review of current studies on this student population.

## INTRODUCTION

Thirty to forty years ago, first-generation college students were predominantly white, working class, baby-boomers whose parents were often first and second generation European immigrants. Over the past three decades demographic changes in race, ethnicity, language and socioeconomic levels have changed the face and cultural experiences of today's first-generation students. This article seeks to examine past and present first-generation college students, how they have changed—or not changed—and what colleges can do to assist them in meeting with success in higher education. Before discussing recent studies on this topic, this article begins with a description of one first-generation student attending college in the 1960s and 70s.

## MY STORY

"Stay in school!" These were words of advice often spoken by my father. He wanted me to have a better life, as most parents do. But he did not have to push me in that direction. Since I first entered school in 1956, I always enjoyed school life, for the most part. Raised in a predominantly Italian, Irish, and Catholic neighborhood, I never realized how poor I was because we were all poor. In this tight-knit, working class neighborhood in East Boston, most families had two parents and while the mother cared for the family and home, the father was the sole source of financial support. I played and went to school with the same children, so there was a deep sense of belonging. For the most part, we all got along, playing simple street games "until dark" on summer nights and "until dinner" on school nights.

I attended the Catholic grammar school across the street from my house. It was a small, poor parish school serviced by the Sisters of Notre Dame, a congregation of religious women who originated in France and Belgium and who came to the United States for the purpose of teaching in

Dr. Corinne R. Merritt is an Assistant Professor of Education at Emmanuel College. She holds a B.A. in Music, an M.Ed. in School Administration, and an Ed.D. from Graduate School of Education Leadership in Urban Schools Program from the University of Massachusetts Boston, as well as an M.Ed. in Creative Arts in Learning from Lesley University.

such schools. The sisters taught us using traditional methods of rote memory and testing, a system commonly employed in the 1950s and 60s. I blossomed in this environment because I clearly understood what was expected of me and I enjoyed the loving atmosphere created by the sisters. In essence, I thrived in this poor but amicable setting.

As I entered preadolescence, I began to explore my world with my friends, many of whom were boys my age. Taking many risks, I learned to swim by jumping off abandoned piers, former ports for the ferry connecting East Boston to "the mainland" downtown Boston. I slid under turnstile bars to catch a free ride on the public subway system and traveled to Revere Beach, quite a distance for an eleven-year-old. One summer day, with little to do, we made a game of "ringing and running," a mischievous task of randomly ringing doorbells and running away. Someone called the police, and I was eventually brought home to my parents where they administered a grave punishment of no dinner and an evening alone in my bedroom to think about what I had done. That evening I heard my mother discussing my behavior with my father. "We have to move, Jay." My dad's name was John, but she called him Jay. "She is getting too wild. The *police* brought her home…what next!"

Later that summer, my mother found a large apartment for rent in a two family house in a much nicer area of Boston. And so, I found myself alone, separated from my friends by what seemed like a continent, in the Dorchester Lower Mills area. I was no longer surrounded by familiar friends and families. The homes were much bigger with bigger yards, and no one played in the streets. In fact, I never realized any children lived in the area until I enrolled in a new school that September. The only consolation to this traumatic change was that the new school, again a Catholic school, was taught by the same

sisters. So I began grade 7, knowing only one person, a sister who was transferred from the school in East Boston to the new school in Dorchester. I slowly changed from an adventurous, curious young girl into a very unhappy, lonely adolescent. In spite of such changes and isolation, I managed to maintain success in school, academically at least.

This new school was much larger than my other school. There were about fifty students in each classroom and three of every grade, kindergarten through grade 8. Most students had Irish surnames and had already well-established social groups; actually they were tight-knit cliques. For a newcomer, especially someone with such strong Italian ethnic connections, it was nearly impossible to form new friends. It was during this time that I began to stay home more and more and, consequently, focused my excess time on playing the piano. I had already had several years of private piano lessons at my former school, but now I was more focused than ever. What else was there to do!

In addition to facing this isolation, I felt different in many other ways. To begin with, I ate very different foods than my peers. They took peanut butter and jelly or tuna sandwiches in their lunch, while I had cold Italian meatloaf or salami and cheese sandwiches, which saturated the air with strong scents of garlic and spices. The girls were, of course, very pretty with long blonde or auburn hair and blue eyes, while I had dark brown hair, brown eyes, and was, shall I say, rather "chubby." Many of my classmates were picked up after school by their parents in very nice cars. My parents could not afford a car, so we took public transportation. The longer the isolation lasted, the more I felt disconnected and worthless.

Now, you might ask yourself, how could she call herself poor if she attended Catholic schools and had private piano lessons? Yes, this might seem ironic, but in the

50s, school tuition was less than $100 per year and piano lessons ranged from $0.75 to $1.00 for a half hour lesson depending on your level of proficiency.

There were other factors which widened the gap between me and many of my peers. Both my parents were first generation American born. My mother's parents came to the U.S. from Italy with little money, and the only skill my grandfather had was as a laborer, fixing roofs, minor plumbing and other odd jobs. When my maternal grandmother died suddenly in a tragic fire, my mother as the oldest of seven was forced to leave school in 10th grade and go to work to help support the family. With her limited language and math skills, she insisted that I put forth my best effort in all my school work. She was a hard-working, family-oriented woman who wanted the best for her family.

Born in Boston, my father was raised by a single-mother who arrived in the U.S. from Russia in early 1917 during the Russian Revolution. My paternal grandmother never learned to speak English and found it difficult to find work and support her family. Growing up in the West End of Boston, my father was exposed to many immigrant groups from Eastern Europe who settled in Boston in the 1920s and 30s. He had a gift for language and consequently became fluent in several Slavic languages, as well as Yiddish. As a young man, my father was very adventurous, so after completing high school he enlisted in the Merchant Marines. He traveled from port to port visiting many cities in North, South and Central America. This was his only educational experience beyond high school. After marrying my mother in 1949, he landed a job as a machinist, making steel components for ships. His company received several contracts from the U. S. Navy which guaranteed his job for some 25 years. Although my father was also hard-working and family-oriented, he was fun-loving, even mischievous—unlike my mother who was much more serious. My father was a jokester and could lighten up any room.

After taking the Catholic High School Entrance Exam, I was accepted to several prestigious Catholic high schools in the greater Boston area. But my parents could not afford the cost of tuition, so I attended the local parish high school for girls. Classes were large and students were separated into one of three tracks, depending on abilities. There was the college-prep track, which I was in, the business track for those girls who planned to work as secretaries or in some form of clerical work, and the "basic" track for those girls who struggled academically. After graduation, many of the "basic" track students went directly to work in such establishments as the Boston Gas Company or the New England Telephone Company. Some of the students in the business track might attend a two year business school before landing an office job. The rest of us were primed for higher education.

In tenth grade we all took a battery of achievement tests which suggested academic and career options based on individual strengths. Our guidance counselor, Sr. Gail, invited each student into her office to discuss the results and to assist us in determining our future plans. "It's too bad you're not a boy!" "Why?" I asked. "Well, these tests indicate that you would be very successful as an architect or some kind of engineer. It's too bad. You would probably do well at some place like Wentworth Institute or an architecture school." And so it was, in the early 60s for many young women, our choices were limited to nursing, secretarial work, or teaching. It was years later that I realized that, had I been raised in a different socioeconomic setting, the choice to be an architect or engineer as a woman would have been quite possible. But, as the product of a lower economic background, I felt limited to those professions suitable for the working class in spite of numerous role models: two hard-working parents, peers who persevered in their academic achievements and teachers who were all white women.

At home, my parents encouraged me not only to pursue a college degree but also to pursue a field of my choice. They supported my efforts but, lacking a college experience themselves, they were ill-equipped to provide advice. I began undergraduate school with the intention of majoring in math. As a freshman, I recall seeking the advice of the chair of the math department, a middle-aged bachelor who responded with a perplexed look. "Why do you want to major in mathematics? That is a discipline for men!" I froze in my seat. I thought as chair of the program he would encourage me to move forward. Instead, I found myself lost in pursuit of a major that would be more suitable for a woman. In time I found my niche as a music major at the public university. Most of my professors were white men who had earned their doctorate degrees at Harvard University and Stanford and who encouraged me through the program. Nearing graduation I wondered what I would do with a bachelor's degree in music. My advisor recommended that I stay at the college one more year and become licensed to teach music. Again I was confronted with conflicting ideas. Of course I loved the idea of staying in school another year; college had been such a rewarding experience for me on many levels—academically and socially. But I never thought of myself as a teacher—I never liked teaching children. I found myself one year later teaching at one of the suburban high schools just outside Boston. I discovered that as much as I loved my discipline, I also had the right personality and skills for working with adolescents. I began teaching the next fall and have been teaching ever since.

This is the story of one first-generation college graduate, but things have changed for today's undergraduates who are the first in their families to attend college. The following section focuses on current studies of first-generation college students, not only providing significant findings, but also providing the reader with practical suggestions for easing the transition for these newcomers into the world of higher education.

## RECENT STUDIES

Byrd and MacDonald (2005) conducted a qualitative study of eight participants, all of whom were first-generation college students, to identify specific characteristics and skills relevant to college readiness. Based on data from interviews, journals and field notes, ten themes emerged which the researchers classified as college readiness skills and abilities, background factors, or student self-concept. Participants revealed four themes representing specific skills and abilities needed to succeed as first-generation college students: academic skills, time management skills, identification and focus on a goal, and ability to self-advocate. Academic skills included reading, writing, math, technology, communication, and study skills. Surprisingly, first-generation students indicated a greater need to arrive in college with reading skills than writing skills. Participants described having problems with vocabulary and realizing the amount of time required to complete reading requirements. Time management skills included balancing studying with work, family, activities and social life. Furthermore, data revealed the necessity to arrive at college having a goal and focusing efforts to achieve that goal. Finally, age and maturity contributed to the ability to speak up for one's needs and to seek help as necessary.

The researchers' (Byrd & MacDonald, 2005) discussion of background factors revealed four themes: family factors, career influences, financial concerns, and college preparation. Among family factors, participants indicated family expectations and experiences as direct influences on their decision to attend college, as well as the desire to do better than their parents, having witnessed how much their parents struggled economically. Work experiences and career aspirations also influenced this decision. Issues around finances suggest the need for first-generation college students to be aware of financial aid and scholarship opportunities. Advanced placement courses taken in high school were the only courses participants identified as helping prepare them for college.

In the last category, the researchers (Byrd & MacDonald, 2005) identified two themes: self-concept and college system. Older students, those who had attended community colleges prior to four year colleges or who took time to pursue possible careers, had more strength in self-concept, self-advocacy, goal focus, and time management than traditional students. The researchers felt non-traditional students were more prepared and ready for the college experience than they thought. Finally, participants indicated the need to understand the college system, college standards, and the culture of the college, and that lacking this knowledge put them at a disadvantage. As supportive as families were, they were not able to offer direction or advice because they themselves had not attended college.

In a longitudinal study of first-generation college students over a three year period, Pascarella, Pierson, Wolniak, and Terenzini (2004) determined a number of factors contributing to student learning and cognitive development. Discussion included the fact that first-generation college students lack the cultural and social capital necessary for making a smooth transition from secondary education. In spite of this, the researchers recognized that these students often acquire greater cultural and social capital than their peers who have one or both parents who were college graduates and who arrive at college with some guidance and possible experiences contributing to cultural and social capital.

Findings were arranged in three categories: college experiences, college outcomes, and conditional effects (Pascarella et al., 2004). The first finding involving college experiences determined that first-generation college students exhibited significant deficit in their choice of college, whereas their peers had the guidance of their parents who were college graduates to advise them. Many first-generation college students held part-time jobs, often working more than 20 hours per week, completed fewer credit hours than their peers, were more likely to live off campus, and consequently, were less apt to become involved in extracurricular activities, clubs and organizations. Growing evidence suggested that extracurricular involvement and interaction with peers contribute to both intellectual and personal development during college (Pascarella et al., 2004).

In the area of college outcomes, researchers (Pascarella et al., 2004) found that over time and with persistence the gaps in writing skills, reading comprehension, critical thinking, and quantitative reasoning lessened between first-generation college students and their peers. Several additional findings were classified as conditional effects. Social and cultural capital acquired during college for first-generation college students resulted from their level of engagement with social and peer networks at the college. Furthermore, involvement in extracurricular activities had positive effects on critical thinking, plans for advanced degrees, self-confidence and control over academic success, and tasks involving higher order thinking. Researchers (Pascarella et al., 2004) found similar positive effects for first-generation college students involved in non-academic related interactions with peers on quantitative reasoning, writing skills, as well as future degree plans. Pascarella et al. concluded that social interaction with peers both within and outside courses, along with extracurricular activities, contributed to gains in social and cultural capital, as well as academic advancements.

In a more recent study utilizing the *College Student Experiences Questionnaire (CSEQ)*, Lundberg, Schreiner, Hovaguimian, and Miller (2007) used a random sample of 4501 undergraduate students, an equal number of 643 students from seven racial and ethnic groups, to discover where students applied effort and what they learned from the college experience. The researchers conjectured that educational and social involvement of first-generation college students led to academic and personal gains and discovered that race and ethnicity had mostly positive effects on involvement. Lundberg et al. defined involvement as use of library, computers and other technologies, course learning, writing, faculty interactions, involvement in fine arts, clubs and organizations, personal experiences and peer interactions, science and quantitative experiences, and discussion of topics and integration of ideas. African American, Native American and some Hispanic students were less involved in campus experiences. Mexican American students were the only ethnic group with a positive effect on personal learning gains and were most likely to interact and to engage in discussions with students unlike themselves. Asian and Pacific Islander students needed encouragement to engage in public discourse; however, the researchers also speculated this could be a result of cultural appropriateness (Lundberg et al., 2007).

Similar to Lundberg et al. (2007), Pike and Kuh (2005) found successful gains for first-generation college students resulted from academic and social engagement and the college environment. First-generation students were less engaged and less likely to integrate diverse college experiences than peers whose parents were college graduates. Female and minority students who lived on campus were more likely to be involved in college life and reported greater gains in their learning and intellectual development than other first-generation students who commuted (Pike & Kuh, 2005).

## CONCLUSION

Research suggests that colleges establish programs to assist first-generation college students adjust to college (Folger, Carter, & Chase, 2004; Gibbons & Shooner, 2004; Laden, 2004; Lundberg et al., 2007; Pascarella et al., 2004; Pike & Kuh, 2005). Summer enrichment programs led by peer groups on college campuses provide guidance to incoming first-generation students on how to manage academic and social demands and on the importance of building relationships with faculty (Folger et al., 2004; Gibbons & Shooner, 2004; Laden, 2004, Lundberg et al., 2007). Lundberg et al. (2007) detail specific recommendations for instituting summer programs that orientate first-generation students and regularly meet with the students throughout the academic year to discuss their progress and needs. Furthermore, the researchers suggest enlightening the teaching faculty on the specific needs of this population of students and how they can assist these students in such areas as class participation and peer collaboration.

Laden (2004) stated specific recommendations for colleges to assist racially diverse student populations in making successful transition to the culture of higher education.

- Colleges should acknowledge and integrate the culture and experiences diverse populations bring to the campus.
- Colleges should create inclusive, comprehensive techniques for curriculum, instructional practices and student services that support academic and social needs.

- Colleges should provide direction for first-generation college students to learn the college system and to make use of such resources as financial aid, writing and academic support services, tutoring services and peer assistance programs.
- Colleges should cultivate a system devoted to early detection of academic, financial, or other concerns that might stand in the way of success for first-generation students.
- Colleges should seek to hire administrators, faculty, and staff representative of the student demographics who could be role models, mentors and advisors.
- Finally, colleges should explore ways for the concerns, ideas, and views of this population to be heard and integrated as part of college life (Laden, 2004).

There are some similarities and some differences between the current group of first generation college students and my generation who were the first in their families to attend college—with race/ethnicity and language being the biggest differences. But, for those of us who teach today's college students, we must keep in mind "how it was" for us and give today's first generation college students the support and understanding they need in order to succeed academically and in their future endeavors.

REFERENCES

Byrd, K. L., & Macdonald, G. (2005). Defining college readiness from the inside out: First-generation college student perspectives. *Community College Review, 33*(1), 22-30.

Folger, W. A., Carter, J. A., & Chase, P. B. (2004). Supporting first generation college freshmen with small group intervention. College *Student Journal, 38*(3), 27-35.

Gibbons, M. M., & Shoffner, M. F. (2004). Prospective first-generation college students: Meeting their needs through social cognitive career theory. *Professional School Counseling, 8*(1), 91-97.

Laden, B. V. (2004). Serving emerging majority students. *New Directions for Community Colleges, 127*, 5-19.

Lundberg, C. A., Schreiner, L. A., Hovaguimian, K. D., & Miller, S. S. (2007). First-generation status and student race/ethnicity as distinct predictors of student involvement and learning. *National Association of Student Personnel Administrators, 44*(1), 57-83.

Pascarella, E. T., Pierson, C. T., Wolniak, G. C., & Terenzini, P. T. (2004). First-generation college students: Additional evidence on college experiences and outcomes. *Journal of Higher Education, 75*(3), 249-284.

Pike, G. R., & Kuh, G. D. (2005). First- and second-generation college students: A comparison of their engagement and intellectual development. *Journal of Higher Education, 76*(3), 276-292.

# Promoting Nursing Workforce Diversity on an Urban Campus

## Linda G. Dumas, Theodore Trevens and Pamela Katz Ressler

*University of Massachusetts Boston*

linda.dumas@umb.edu • ted.trevens@umb.edu • pressler@stressresources.com

**Abstract:** The Nursing Scholars Program at the University of Massachusetts Boston's (UMass) College of Nursing and Health Sciences (CNHS) promotes enrollment, retention, and post-graduation success for minority and economically disadvantaged nursing students. As discussed below, this is a federally funded HRSA Workforce Diversity grant. The program consists of many activities: peer group meetings, community-based cultural competency trainings, leadership education, program advisors, a community space, laptop computers, ESL classes, tutors, and scholarships or stipends for eligible students. This article is intended to provide an overview of our methods and practices, how we incorporated student feedback into our model, and our unique approach to outsourcing evaluation (singled out by HRSA as a particular strength of our grant proposal), as well as our recommendations to others considering a similar model.

The Nursing Scholars Program at the University of Massachusetts Boston's (UMass) College of Nursing and Health Sciences (CNHS) promotes enrollment, retention, and post-graduation success for minority and economically disadvantaged nursing students. As discussed below, this is a federally funded HRSA Workforce Diversity grant. The program consists of many activities: peer group meetings, community-based cultural competency trainings, leadership education, program advisors, a community space, laptop computers, ESL classes, tutors, and scholarships or stipends for eligible students.

This article is intended to provide an overview of our methods and practices, how we incorporated student feedback into

Linda Dumas PhD RN ANP- BC is an Associate Professor in the College of Nursing and Health Sciences at the University of Massachusetts Boston. She is an adult nurse practitioner in long term care and holds an MA and PhD in Sociology. Her research is focused on workforce diversity program development for minority and underrepresented nursing students. She is the principal investigator for the Nursing Scholars Program. Theodore Trevens, MBA has 18 years of experience in the nonprofit sector, including senior management positions with foundations and direct service organizations. He holds an MBA from Boston College, is an expert in nonprofit organizational development and is specifically interested helping nonprofits to adapt private sector methods to improve their effectiveness. He serves as the business manager for the Nursing Scholars Program. Pamela Katz Ressler RN BSN HN-BC is founder and president of Stress Resources in Concord, a firm specializing in stress management program development. Pam is a lecturer and consultant to the Nursing Scholars Program, and develops stress resiliency training models for the NSP undergraduate students and the College of Nursing and Health Sciences. She is a frequent public speaker on mind body medicine and healing arts in health care.

our model, and our unique approach to outsourcing evaluation (singled out by HRSA as a particular strength of our grant proposal), as well as our recommendations to others considering a similar model.

## COMMUNITY NEED

The Nursing Scholars Program exists to fill a documented need in both the medical and academic communities.

Minorities are underrepresented in the nursing profession. Despite the fact that minority groups comprise almost 33% of the U.S. population, only 12.3% of registered nurses represent racial or ethnic minority groups.[1] In nursing programs in Massachusetts there is a tremendous lack of minorities enrolled and graduating. In fact, "At Boston hospitals up to 95% of housekeeping staff and 80% of food services workers are minorities. But the number of registered nurses who are minorities is less than 10% in most institutions."[2] And even though CNHS has a much higher rate of minority enrollment, as well as a higher rate of minority graduates, than the rest of the state, its enrollment still does not adequately reflect the diversity of minorities in the local community.

To make matters worse, in 2005 Massachusetts had a shortfall of 4,820 nurses, or 7%. By 2010 this shortfall is projected to reach 12% and to continue growing.[3] This shortage is different from past nursing shortages, because the workforce is getting older, thereby shrinking the overall workforce as they retire.[4] At the same time, young people are choosing not to enter the

nursing profession because they have better career options. For current nurses, there are a number of workplace problems including excessive workloads, inadequate staffing, and workplace safety issues.[5] All of these factors will contribute to a shortage of nurses in the Boston area for the foreseeable future.

Retention rates for minority students at CNHS lagged behind those for white students from 2000 to 2004, with rates for minorities hitting a low of 51% in 2001-2002.[6] In the past, NCLEX passing rates for whites overwhelmed the scores of all minorities with only 8% of whites failing the examination.

Faced with this community need—the documented nursing workforce shortage, under-representation of minorities in the nursing community, and lagging NCLEX passing and retention rates of minority students at UMass—we applied for and received funding from the United States Department of Health and Human Services Health Resource and Services Administration (HRSA) Bureau of Health Professions Nursing Workforce Diversity Program for two grants. The first was the Bringing the Best to Nursing (BBN) Program (2003-2006), and our current grant is the Nursing Scholars Program [NSP] (2007-2010).

## HRSA FUNDING

We are now in the process of administering our second HRSA-funded Nursing Workforce Diversity Grant. Bringing the Best to Nursing ran from 2003 to 2006 and enrolled 114 students. To date, 50 BBN stu-

[1] Baldwin, D. (2003, January 31.). *Disparities in Health and Health Care: Focusing Efforts to Eliminate Unequal Burdens*. Online Journal of Issues in Nursing. Vol. #8 No. #1.
[2] Rowland, C. (2006, August 5.). Hospitals Move to Boost Skilled Workers, *Boston Globe*.
[3] Ensuring an Educated Nursing Workforce for the Commonwealth, Massachusetts Association of Colleges of Nursing (MACN). (2005).

[4] Sroczynski, M. (2003, January.). The Nursing Faculty Shortage: A Public Health Crisis, The Nursing Career Ladder Initiative. NUCLI State Advisory Committee.
[5] Massachusetts Colleagues in Caring Collaborative. (2002). The 2001 Massachusetts Workforce Survey-Executive Summary.
[6] UMASS. The Office of Institutional Research and Policy Studies. (2004). *One Year Retention Rates for Fall Entrants 1998-2004 Cohorts*.

dents have graduated, which is a 100% retention rate. Among the other documented successes of the BBN program are the "culture of community" noted by students as being essential to improving academic experience, retention and performance; the "advocacy model" of advising, where students appreciated faculty attention and assistance; and the Diversity Training Workshops, led by minority nurses.

The Nursing Scholars Program received its HRSA funding in Fall of 2007. Twenty-one students were enrolled in Fall 2007, and 30 in Spring 2008. The objectives of the Nursing Scholars Program are as follows:

1. Improve access to the nursing profession for disadvantaged students and underrepresented populations;
2. Increase culturally responsive, excellent health care by diverse nurses to diverse populations;
3. Demonstrate the efficacy of a rigorous student nurse retention program that is framed by a "Culture of Community" learning model;
4. Enhance faculty knowledge and sensitivity around cultural competence, student support, and diversity in underrepresented, at risk students;
5. Collaborate with Health Careers Opportunities Program at UMass to introduce Nursing as a career to minority children and their families;
6. Provide stipends, scholarships and laptop computers to students to introduce computers into their education.

The Nursing Scholars Program grew out of lessons learned from the BBN grant. NSP participants are recruited from the cohort of incoming CNHS students as well as from current CNHS freshmen and sophomores. NSP students need to meet the requirements of the college for acceptance into nursing school and must be in the Bachelor of Science degree program. Stu-

dents accepted into the school have at least a 2.75 GPA and have passed the TOEFL (English Proficiency) examination. Graduate students and students who are registered nurses (RN) who have returned to get their baccalaureate degree are not included. Students may enter NSP at any time after completing their pre-nursing courses (sophomore year for undergraduates and upon entry for transfer students). Thirty new students are accepted into the NSP each semester. They formally attend the program for three semesters and receive support from the program until they graduate.

In order to join the program, students submit their most recent transcripts and complete a two-page NSP application, which is then reviewed by the NSP Enrollment Committee. The Committee includes the Program Director and the Faculty Advisors. The application requires an essay on nursing goals and a short essay on how NSP will benefit the student and what the student will bring to the program. Students at greatest risk of not completing the degree and/or not passing their board examination are given first priority for inclusion in the program. The Committee evaluates the student's risk by ranking factors collected in the application, such as obligations outside of the program, English language skills (ESL/writing proficiency exam), grade point average, financial stressors, etc. The resulting index is then monitored and evaluated through our database on a semester-by-semester basis, and as the need is otherwise determined, in order to ensure that adequate support is given to this population of students. All students must be minority and/or economically disadvantaged per the federal definitions accepted at the time of enrollment into NSP. All applicants must verify possession of a visa permitting permanent residence in the United States; or prove they are U.S. citizens, non-citizen nationals, or foreign nationals.

The panel also looks for a student's interest in serving an area that is experiencing the most critical nursing shortages, such working with minority populations or in long-term care. Following is the order of priority for NSP enrollment:

- Minority/economically disadvantaged (requirement);
- Identified as at-risk (as ranked by Committee);
- Nursing goals (subjective, with areas in most critical need to receive priority);
- Obligations outside of school;
- ESL exam and English skills.

## NURSING SCHOLARS PROGRAM (NSP)

The program is based on a small learning community model. Once accepted into the program, all NSP students are assigned to one of the four NSP advisors, whom they are required to see once a semester, and to stay in touch with by phone or email at least once a month. The advisors are dedicated members of the CNHS faculty who serve students in addition to the students' university advisor. The NSP advisor assists with class schedules, time and life management issues, planning for NCLEX, navigating UMass administrative systems, and other issues that affect the students' ability to succeed at UMass. Advisors also help students close to graduation on professional development, networking, and other job search issues. Advisors keep written records of meetings with students and enter them into our database to track effectiveness of the program. This database will have the functionality of e-mailing students a detailed report of topics discussed during the advising session and action items for the student. These reports are also used to keep students accountable for their academic and professional development. The advisors work with the advising coordinator to identify problems early so that stu-

dents can find support in overcoming whatever challenges they face.

Feedback from BBN students found BBN advisors to be much more responsive to student needs than university advisors. BBN advisors were able to make an impact because they were CNHS faculty and because students were more comfortable with them than with someone who functions more broadly as an academic advisor. BBN advisors also actively pursued relationships with students, assuring students that they were not only a problem-solver but also a means of support. They also made themselves more available to visit with students.

## PEER GROUPS

Peer groups are held each month. Each NSP student is assigned to a group of 8-10 students. Attendance is required and is recorded, as are topics discussed. Faculty members in charge choose the topics to be discussed. Peer Group Leaders meet regularly to identify what issues are relevant to the students, what is going on in specific groups, and what strategies are working within the groups. During the NS senior year, peer groups transition to optional student-led groups. The data from this regular forum are used to capture, analyze, and incorporate feedback from participants into the ongoing enhancement of the program.

## TUTORING

Graduate and peer tutors are available to students to assist with homework and exam preparation. Students are referred by their advisor for tutoring or they request it based on their own perceived needs at any time. Tutoring sessions are coordinated by a CHNS faculty member who assigns an undergraduate work study peer tutor. An indicator is placed in the database upon each tutorial visit to provide a basis of comparison between students who take advantage of tutoring and those who do not. Analyses will be run using the risk index and GPA alone on a per semester basis. The assumption is that students who avail themselves of tutoring and other forms of academic support will perform better and be at a lower risk for attrition and poor NCLEX performance.

## SEMINARS

Students in the NSP have the opportunity to attend an ongoing seminar series that focuses on six topics: Study Smarter Not Harder, Quick Relaxation Tools for Nurses, Stress Resiliency, Effective Communication, Caring for the Caregivers and Resonant Leadership for Nurses. These seminars focus on developing leadership and study skills and addressing the general issues faced by the NS students, as identified in pilot BBN focus groups. The seminar series was developed by a nurse who specializes in presenting workshops nationally on stress reduction and effective study habits. The seminars are held several times, at different times during the day and on different days of the week to ensure that students will be able to attend. All seminars are evaluated by students through written surveys and during peer group discussions.

## COMMUNITY MENTORS

Students are matched with a mentor in the nursing field who can give advice and career guidance. Mentors have a broad array of skills and experiences because of the nature of health care in Boston. For example, students might be matched with nurses who specialize in community settings, academic settings, or nurses who have expertise in a particular immigrant population. The mentors include minority nurses and nurses who are multi-lingual.

This program is coordinated by a graduate assistant who works in conjunction with the Faculty Coordinator. NSP staff has developed a roster of enthusiastic and committed nurse mentors from community hospitals including Massachusetts General Hospital, Caritas St. Elizabeth's Medical Center, and the Dana-Farber Cancer Institute. A written agreement signed by the two parties ensures understanding of expectations from the outset of the mentorship. Success of the mentoring partnership is measured by the objectives met as described in this agreement. Our database tracks the impact mentoring relationships have over the long-term in regard to employment, salary and career development.

This program component also figures prominently in the monthly peer group meeting discussions. Talking about the mentoring experiences allows discussion leaders to offer tips and techniques on getting the most out of the mentoring relationship. These discussions may also encourage other students to pursue a mentoring relationship.

## ENGLISH AS A SECOND LANGUAGE (ESL) CLASSES

Lack of English language skills is at the root of many of the issues being faced by nursing students. English is not the first language for the majority of CNHS students. ESL coaches, students who are further along in the program and speak the same language as the students to whom they are assigned, assist students with their school work and other issues. Coaches meet weekly with students and are supervised in monthly meetings by ESL Faculty at UMass.

## COMPUTERS

Students are loaned a laptop computer and a printer for personal use during their enrollment in the program. CNHS currently has 40 computers and printers that were used as part of BBN. These computers were upgraded and are now used as part of the NS program.

Since knowledge and competence of computer operation is standard in the medical field, providing this technology and training helps students who are not computer literate feel more comfortable using the computers. Individuals who already are computer literate have the opportunity to refine their skills. The computers are equipped with a wireless card for Internet access, Microsoft Office software, and NCLEX and Medical Terminology software with an instructional CD-ROM. Classes are available at the start of each semester for the students to be trained in use of this software. Additional support is available through the CNHS library, where training modules are available, and through a variety of the CNHS courses that enhance computer skills.

## STIPEND

NSP participants receive either a stipend or a tuition waiver of $800 per semester, for up to three semesters of the program. To qualify, students must remain in the NSP program and meet the income guidelines according to the definition of economically disadvantaged students provided by the U.S. Bureau of Census at the time of application. All students receive the same amount whether it is a stipend or a scholarship. All students who receive the stipend or scholarship must be enrolled on a full-time basis.

While students are not required to detail where the funds are spent, this information is asked informally using an on-line student reporting tool, as well as during peer group sessions. Data that are gathered through these methods are tracked in the database in order to assess the impact on

the risk index and other important persistence predictors.

## PRE-ENTRY PREPARATION PROGRAM

NSP has created a nursing education pipeline from middle school through graduate school by providing nursing-specific outreach to middle and high school students through the UMass Health Careers Opportunity Program (HCOP). Each year HCOP serves approximately 300 middle and high school students enrolled in the UMass Pre-Collegiate and Educational Support Programs: Urban Scholars, Upward Bound, Math Science Upward Bound, Project REACH, Admission Guaranteed, and GEAR-UP. All HCOP activities are designed to encourage economically and educationally disadvantaged Boston Public School students to pursue a career in a health profession.

To attract students, HCOP disseminates program information to parents, teachers, guidance counselors and other personnel at the target middle and high schools, to community groups and agencies and through direct mailings to students and parents. Interested students are invited to general information sessions hosted by HCOP. Among those who participate, HCOP identifies and recruits students interested in nursing.

NSP provides support within all HCOP programs, which are organized around three main areas: early awareness, preparation and planning, and facilitating entry. HCOP's early awareness activities introduce about 300 students per year to information about the wide variety of jobs in the health and public health fields. HCOP offers after-school and summer academic classes and tutorial support to ensure that the pre-collegiate students have a strong foundation in subjects required for a nursing (or other health-related) degree such as math, science, and critical thinking.

In addition, HCOP will convene a Nursing Careers Club in which 20 students in grades 10-12 meet two times a week after school. Students receive tutoring, take field trips to health-related organizations, research nursing careers, receive CPR training, present their findings to peers and parents, and are matched with a current NS student mentor. Students in the club receive weekly stipends of $25 for attending the club. Parents are encouraged to be involved with their children's pursuit of the nursing career and are regularly invited to attend club events and activities. With the support of HCOP and to facilitate the transition from secondary to higher education, each club member participates in individualized college advising and awareness activities. Students learn about higher education, the college admissions process, and financial aid through presentations by university departments, guest speakers, college recruiters, seminars, college visits, and one-on-one advising. HCOP staff work with students and parents to oversee the students' admission process in partnership with the NSP. HCOP participants who matriculate at CNHS are guaranteed admission into the NSP.

## NSP/BBN

Through the experience of administering our BBN, we learned a number of lessons and valuable principles which we have subsequently applied to the NSP. For example, we kept the advising advocacy model, the monthly peer groups, the peer tutoring, and the small community learning model. In addition, the ongoing facilitation of peer support, the culture of community throughout, and the physical aspects of the program—the university space, lounges, NSP office, and computers and training—are all components of the BBN program which we have maintained.

However, many things have changed. The youth program component (the partnership with the HCOP), seminar series, and optional mentoring with community mentors are new additions to the program, and we have developed stronger outcome monitoring, training, tracking and technical assistance with help from our evaluation consultant. Additional programmatic changes are made each year based on actual outcomes.

## DATA MANAGEMENT AND MONITORING

NSP is constantly working to collect data that will improve the effectiveness of the program. Our evaluation methods and data collection allow us to identify which elements of the retention activities are delivering the highest benefits to our students, thereby enabling us to find better ways to serve disadvantaged students. By highlighting the components of our program that are working best and by providing specific cost data on the delivery of these components, we can work with the CNHS to integrate these methods into the college. This is being done with the support of the school since the pilot BBN was viewed as fertile ground for fostering innovative strategies and developing a vital learning community for our future nurses. As NSP progresses, the successful aspects will be integrated into the university, after federal funding ends in 2010.

An outside consultant has designed and implemented a database system and trained NSP staff on its use. Additionally, NSP is provided with ongoing maintenance, training, and technical assistance. The result is an outcome-based monitoring cycle integrated with the UMass mainframe, which collects in-depth and focused information about NSP students, their activities and experiences. NSP faculty members now have data at their fingertips when making important programmatic changes, adjustments and implementations.

Data will be reported in weekly, monthly, semester, annual, and longitudinal reports. Graduates of the program are followed closely at one, three, and five years post-graduation.

## SUMMARY

Over 70 BBN program graduates are currently working as nurses, primarily in urban areas with high minority and economically disadvantaged populations. In the next two semesters BBN students will continue to graduate and join the workforce. After funding for the Nursing Scholars program ends, CNHS is committed to incorporating proven successful methods into the overall nursing program. As NSP's racially and economically disadvantaged candidates graduate and become nurses, the program will be shown to have provided a diverse nursing work force and to have assured that a supply of nurses is available to minority patients in Boston. NSP will further graduate nurses who can ensure quality of care to these populations and improve the public health and health care system by providing an efficient and effective nursing workforce.

# Teach Others to Learn While You Are Learning to Teach

## A Personal Journey in Linking Pedagogy and Technology

**Tara Devi S. Ashok**

*University of Massachusetts Boston*

tara.ashok@umb.edu

**Abstract:** I have found that "teaching others to learn while you are learning to teach" is a good statement of my pedagogy. Teaching began for me in 1983 and is a passion, which happens to overlap with my profession. It is a personal account of this journey that I share in this paper. The narrated experiences are of teaching in India and the United States. My teaching has been greatly enriched by my research in the field of human genetics. It has provided a unique perspective on learning. Some of the questions posed are: Do we have to know whether we can teach before we start to teach? Is learning to teach easy? How does one change one's style of teaching to cope with modern times when digital media has taken over the lives of the new generation? Can we develop personalized teaching? These are a few questions addressed here which are faced by all who want to teach. Is teaching your passion? That is always the first question that needs to be addressed, because if the answer is yes, then all other things fall into place.

*Life is a pilgrimage*
*Be joyous during the arduous journey to the*
*summit*
*For the arduous journey is the daily*
*enlightenment and*
*The summit non-existent.*
　　—Tara, June 4th, 2006

I have found that "teaching others to learn while you are learning to teach" is a good statement of my pedagogy. What better could life offer as a profession? I enumerate here a personal journey of my teaching and pedagogy and its links with modern technology. Teaching is my passion, and

Dr. Tara Devi S. Ashok has a PhD in Anthropology from India, with a specialization in Human Genetics. Her passion has been teaching and research, which she has carried out in India, Europe and the U.S. for more than two decades. The genetics of mental retardation was the starting point of her research in human genetics followed by study of hemoglobinopathies both at clinical and population levels. In the U.S., she started work on mitochondrial DNA. Tara's later research experience in Cancer Genetics at the Harvard School of Public Health (1997-2003), Boston, was of great importance not only for understanding the genetic aspects of cancer, but also for human suffering both at the physical and mental levels. Teaching and research are what she does presently at the University of Massachusetts Boston's Departments of Anthropology and Biology. Having had the opportunity to closely look at health from various angles, she is both an anthropologist and a molecular biologist, above all a keen observer of the mind. She seeks to impart the knowledge that she has gathered over the years in a very simple and direct way, so that all can benefit from her learning.

a large part of my profession. It all began for me in 1983.

*Is teaching your passion?* That is the first question to ask for anyone wanting to teach. It has to come from deep within, just like a lactating mother wanting to release her nourishment to her child. Similarly, the revelation of the truth within oneself and the joy thereof has to be shared. *Is that your situation?*

The development of the passion in oneself is what propels a teacher to teach across culture, discipline, ethnicity, gender, economic stratifications and borders, in order to reach the common human denominator: unique minds who can be motivated. Sharing is as limitless as it is joyous. This gives a sense of freedom to the self and is thus self-liberating. Is it then loaded with responsibility? Are you ready for the challenge? Challenge, which tells you to first know the truth and then lead others to that truth?

Today, teaching is done in many ways using different forms of technology. I find all those very fascinating and have incorporated many of the different digital media into my teaching format. I have created computer applications in a style that helps me to express my unique and personalized design for sharing information with the students in a colorful, and animated manner. In most of the situations, this is done with a touch of humor too. These applications complement my lectures and help me to use my research material as examples in these designs. All the animations have been created with the help of the Macromedia Director software.

*The next question is, "Do we have to know whether we can teach before we start to teach?"* No, is my answer, because everyone is capable of teaching. While teaching, you learn many things. That is why my pedagogy is inspired by the motto "teach others to learn while you are learning to teach." Given my disciplinary background, I find biological metaphors sometimes powerful for capturing all that is involved in this process.

The process of developing a teaching strategy is like the development of an embryo, no matter what the stage is of the embryo, it is functional. The heart is beating before the four chambers of the heart are constructed, the nervous system developing, while helping to develop other parts of the body. The germ cells that create the genitals wait in the yolk sac, until the genital ridges are formed, which would be the final destination for these germ cells to reside on after which the sex is determined. But slowly and steadily we function while we build ourselves, unlike a machine that is not switched on until it is completely built.

I find the process of teaching just the same, it grows on us and we go on constructing the parts of teaching while becoming a teacher. Further, present research in biology tells us that we inherit a genome (the genetic component from each of our parents) and an epigenome that makes this genome functional. This epigenome can be influenced by internal and external environmental factors. Similarly, during this phase of becoming a teacher, we are influenced by both our heredity and our environment, and keep changing our teaching style as we respond to the individuals whom we teach.

While I was doing my doctoral thesis on the genetics of mental retardation, I came in close contact with children who were mentally challenged. This brought me to the understanding that everyone does not learn the same way. All of us come with different types of learning capacities, yet all can be taught to bring out the best in themselves. It is very much like the scientists today trying to deliver personalized medicine using the field of pharmacogenomics (i.e., the study of differential drug responses on the basis of individual genetics). This would help physicians prescribe medication suitable to each individual's genetics.

*Will we be able to develop the same kind of teaching strategy, namely, "a personalized teaching"?* Are we ready for this personalized approach? Today, teaching is a big enterprise and done for the masses, many times even over the World Wide Web. So technically all can learn. But, a personalized approach is an ancient approach, which is referred to in India as the Gurukul approach to teaching, like the concept of home schooling in the United States of America. However, in the Gurukul style the students move to the *Guru's* residence and the wife of the *Guru* is like a mother in the house. She serves the students food and takes care of all their requirements and the students have to participate in all the household chores. In this style of education, the students get to observe the *Guru* from close quarters. They are able to see that the *Guru* practices what he preaches. During this period of learning, students have a simple and an austere lifestyle to follow.

I have had the opportunity to teach in two countries namely, India and the U.S. (for more than a decade in each case). Along with this I carried out research work in India, Germany, Netherlands, and the United States. These experiences have greatly enriched my life in more than one way.

*What are the few things I learned from this long travel?* Firstly, that irrespective of where you come from on the world map, a human is a human with the same underlying desires, potentials and aspirations to be the best in as many ways as possible. Secondly, that every culture has a unique influence on the individual. By birth I am an Indian and have been strongly influenced by my culture, but because of my long travels across different countries, it makes me feel like a world citizen today. Humankind truly appears as one. People of all different cultures are the same, human beings. Thirdly, everyone has the desire to learn, but how we cope with the system which provides higher learning is what tells us about the strength of the desire in a person for learning. The ones with the strong desire are able to fight at every step to be on the learners' mode eternally. My exposure to different cultures and the academic curricula of more

than one university has prepared me in trying to teach anyone, anywhere, of any culture or ethnicity. During a lecture, it is possible to combine different methods of teaching, as the goal is basically to teach the mind of the seeker to learn. Sometimes the mindset has to be modified to assure the seeker that learning is possible by a different method. The fear of examination and the fear of expressing one's opinion in a classroom environment has to be overcome so that learning becomes more comfortable and approachable.

Fourthly, the eye contact with all the students during a lecture has become my strength in making my lectures have an interactive nature. To do this the teacher must have the contents of the lecture well organized. This comes naturally when the teacher is engaged in research in the field of the subject being taught. Teaching helped me to keep the basic concepts very clear in my mind and the ongoing research kept my mind healthy and loaded with examples collected from my personal research work. Therefore, all these years, the subject for the students has been kept real. Last but not the least, a touch of humor and media incorporation into simple applications makes a lecture come alive.

*How does one change the style of teaching to cope with modern times when digital media has taken over the lives of the new generation?* A teacher has to keep abreast with the latest technologies that keep coming their way to improve the teaching style. Therefore, my lecturing style has changed over time. Earlier, one had to be an orator to lecture, and write on a blackboard with a white chalk with a beautiful handwriting. The black board then changed to a white one, with colored pens to write with. Then the days of overheads and slides came in, which has been followed by computer presentations of different types. The PowerPoint software today is the most commonly used application. It is equipped with some tools for creation of animation. However, today there are many applications that provide the full range of tools to allow creation of special animations. In 1997, I learned the Director software program, which helped me to create movies. A main menu page is created and many movies can be linked to it. With the help of the various buttons, the student can navigate through the contents of the software application.

Two examples of the main menu page are illustrated below. One for teaching about DNA (deoxyribonucleic acid) and the other to teach all about biological anthropology. Twenty five movies have been linked to these pages and the movies can be played by pressing on the different buttons on the menu bar.

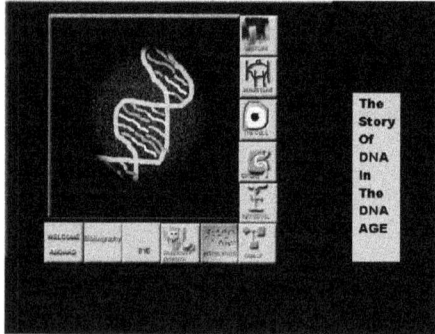

These are the chromosomes of the author seen during cell division. For a human being to be normal he or she should have 46 chromosomes. These are then arranged into a karyotype, by looking at the length and position of the centromeres. Centromere is the part that holds the two arms of a chromosome together.

I could in addition develop games using the Director software for the students to understand some concepts more easily by just playing a simple game.

One example of a game is to arrange the 46 chromosomes in a proper order, based on their size and position of the centromere. This type of arrangement is called a karyo-

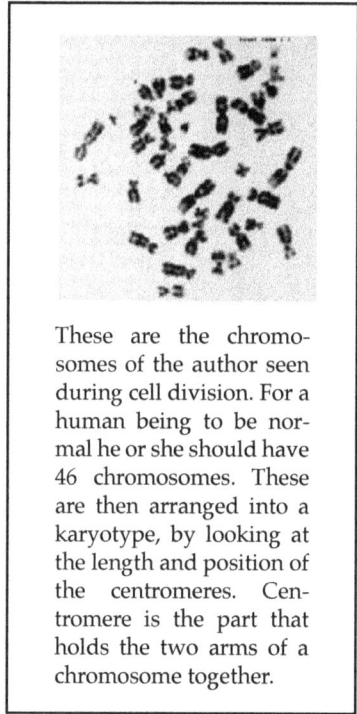

type and the process karyotyping. It is important for the understanding of chromosomal abnormalities in an individual. It can be useful for pre or postnatal diagnosis.

Looking at the given karyotype a student can drag the pair of chromosomes onto the sheet and place it in the right order by looking at the length and position of the centromeres. The longest chromosome is the first one and the shortest being the last. If the lengths are same then the position of the centromeres are considered. The chromosome with the centromere in the center comes first and the chromosome with the centromere above the center come next in line. The numbers indicated on the sheet help in placing the chromosomes on the right location. Karyotyping helps in the understanding of the number, structure and the pattern of the chromosomes. The number and pattern should be the same for all normal individuals. Any change is indicative of an abnormality.

The use of computers and animation have been very fulfilling for me as a teacher.

A Game to learn **KARYOTYPING**

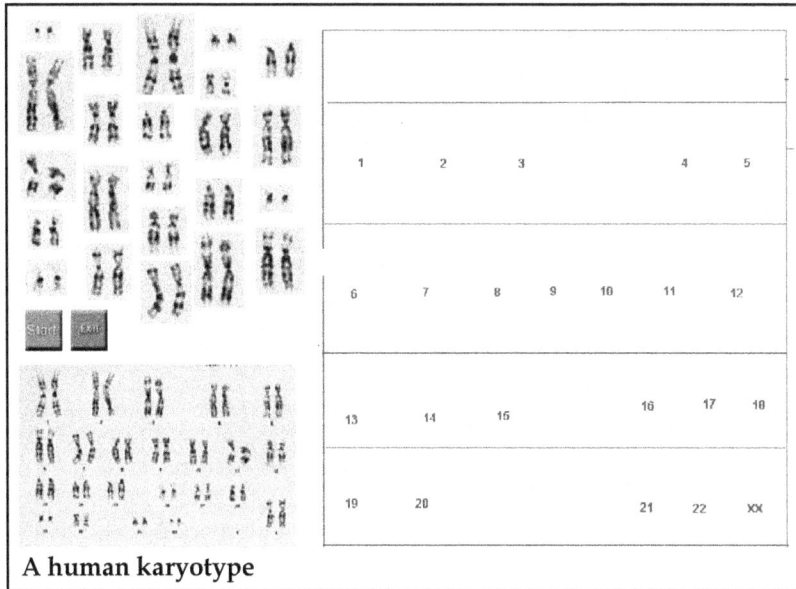

**A human karyotype**

Creativity could be expressed on a daily basis, be it in the creation of an art piece or creation of music. Further, the use of such technologies made my own understanding of science still better, because it requires a thorough knowledge of the subject matter. This made me to go deeper into the basic concepts in all the subjects that I taught. If we want our students to be motivated, we have to be motivated first, or else how can we show the way to learning? With technology, you can learn as you go along, and change the technology with time; otherwise, we become an outdated teacher who is worth her weight in gold, of course, but who does not live in modern times. If we show the fear of learning then how can we preach that learning is easy?

In addition to using computer applications, I found that to teach subjects like biological anthropology and population genetics I wanted the students to actually go to a field station and carry out genetic studies of real populations. This made the students realize how data is collected and analyzed. Each year this fieldwork became tougher in regard to the approach to the populations under study. In 1989, I could study the people of South India who even today live in cave dwellings with wild life all around them in a forest preserve with crystal clear river running through. This field trip was documented in the form of a film entitled, *A Visit to the Cave Dwellers of South India—A Genetic Voyage.* I presented this as a case study for my biological anthropology course and for demonstrating research methodologies in anthropology. On such field trips I used to get the taste of the Gurukul style of teaching, as the teacher and the students both live under the same roof, exploring similar thoughts in the same environment.

Today, teaching can be done for students who are unable to travel long distances to a university. A teacher from one location lectures over the satellite connection to students in different locations. This was the opportunity I was given at Roane State Community College (1996), in Oak Ridge, Tennessee—to teach anatomy and physiology in this manner. What one had to learn was that the students on the other end hear you with a little time delay, say half a minute or so. The television monitors are all connected to allow seeing of the students participating from different locations. Hence, the classroom extended beyond the students sitting right in front of the teacher.

Over these years, I have been able to teach subjects across disciplines, the courses ranging from biological anthropology, biology, human genetics, biochemistry, developmental biology, and developmental models in human evolution, human origins, anthropology of health and illness, population genetics, anatomy, and physiology. This has led me to think truly in a multi-dimensional manner so that I can look at a problem from many angles and understand the biological processes right from a micro or molecular level to the macro level of a complete being. Basically, all the subjects are one in my mind, as all the disciplines contribute equally towards the understanding of the whole.

A few students at the University of Massachusetts Boston have also started to participate in this manner of learning (2003-2008), who have taken many of these courses one after the other, thereby getting the answers to their questions in a holistic way with the help of this interdisciplinary approach.

In India, I taught masters students in the Department of Genetics, Delhi University (1985-1993), who spend two years to complete the masters program. Only five students were registered each year. We had deliberately kept the number low to teach them well. The lecture classes were followed by long hours of laboratory work. Each student received significant personal attention and personal training time in the laboratory. There were no handouts provided and no required textbook as the information had to be collected using many sources. The students pursuing these applied courses were of a high caliber. After they completed the program they went into research and are still doing well in science.

In November of 1993, I arrived at the

U.S., started my research work in the Medical center of Knoxville, Tennessee and within an year started teaching undergraduate students of community colleges. I had moved to the U.S., because of my marriage.

After delivering the first lecture in Knoxville, TN; I realized that I needed to change my way of teaching. These were undergraduate students. I gave out a detailed handout, had a slower lecturing pace, learned to speak English with an American accent. This brought a big smile on the students' faces. They said, "You changed overnight!" I found that fascinating. Thereafter, I have kept improving on my American accent as I find delivering a lecture in the local language is an essential part of teaching. Here, the syllabus for teaching Anatomy and Physiology had been formulated in advance by others faculty members, and I had just to follow it. The number of students in each class was around 35. Using the cadaver to teach Anatomy and Physiology changed my entire perspective on life and teaching in particular.

After spending four years in Tennessee, I moved to Massachusetts and found it to be very different. Tennessee was slow and quiet, whereas Massachusetts was fast paced. Teaching at the University of Massachusetts Boston has also been unique in many ways. I like the ethnic diversity here. The big change came in the number of students that I taught. It ranged from a class having 10 students to a class of 250 students. Hence, in each case I had to develop a different strategy. I prescribed a specific textbook, provided students with detailed handouts and tutoring sessions to make the facts understandable to one and all.

Further, the facts had to be connected to arrive at the truth thereby transforming knowledge into wisdom. This transformation seen in a student is what fills the teacher with great joy and energy that propels the wheels forward for more intensive teaching.

While I was going through the adventures in teaching, I was also involved in carrying out research work in the field of human genetics. I was learning the modern techniques of DNA analysis and seeing the suffering of humans due to genetic disorders. At the same time the computer technology had to be mastered. For me two tracks were going hand in hand, the first one being the unraveling of the knowledge of DNA (deoxyribonucleic acid), and the second, knowledge of computer technology. Both tracks were progressing fast and one day they merged into the fields of Biotechnology and Bioinformatics.

Today, scientific instruments can all be connected directly to a computer, so that results seen in a laboratory can immediately be digitized and projected in a classroom. This allows for teaching to be done in real time in conjunction with the laboratory.

The students in this information age find it very intimidating to assimilate all the information given to them. The teacher's job has become equally difficult. It is here that the digital media comes in handy to explain difficult concepts in a short time as for a student to learn all this at one time is a very big task.

All these years, research and teaching have gone hand in hand, complementing each other at every step of my life. What I look forward to now is teaching over the World Wide Web, where you can practically teach anyone in the world. This is the world that I want to step into. YouTube is a video sharing website where lectures can be upload easily in the form of video clips. Further, I would like to create animations in FLASH software so that they can be uploaded to the web easily. Now, all these technologies help students to have a teacher from any part of the world. It is already a reality.

Today, life has become so fascinating because experiments in science and teaching can be done on a daily basis with the help of cutting edge technologies. But all this information was not available at the time when I began college. There were no personal computers, and very few laboratories were equipped for carrying out work on DNA technology; but what I graduated with, was the capacity to learn on my own. Therefore, today I teach students to just learn to learn. The travel through the times has been so memorable, and the ascent is still going on.

www.ingramcontent.com/pod-product-compliance
Lightning Source LLC
Chambersburg PA
CBHW080402030426
42334CB00024B/2968